#obses:
Instagram Expos

#obsessed
Instagram Exposes Humanity

#obsessed
Instagram Exposes Humanity

#obsessed
Instagram Exposes Humanity
A Crazy & Obsessed Series (Book 2)
Addicted to Instagram

#obsessed
Instagram Exposes Humanity

#obsessed
Instagram Exposes Humanity

#obsessed
Instagram Exposes Humanity
A Crazy & Obsessed Series (Book 2)
Addicted to Instagram

#obsessed
Instagram Exposes Humanity

#obsessed
Instagram Exposes Humanity

Table of Contents

#obsessed
Instagram Exposes Humanity

#obsessed
Instagram Exposes Humanity

#obsessed
Instagram Exposes Humanity

The Dark World of Instagram

"Instagram is a social platform that has been tarnished by the ego of modern society. Instagram is where young hopefuls go to create and crush their dreams."

#love. #instagood. #photooftheday. #fashion. #beautiful. #happy. #cute. #tbt. #like4like. #followme. #picoftheday. #follow. #me. #selfie. #summer. #art. #instadaily. #friends. #repost. #nature. #girl. #fun. #style. #smile. #food.

#obsessed
Instagram Exposes Humanity

According to the latest Instagram "influencer" market, these are the top twenty-five most popular hashtags known to the social media world. However, it doesn't just end there. This list continues to multiply as we come up with new words daily that modern individuals can use to define themselves as "belonging," "prestigious," or better yet, "influencing."

For years, Instagram users have been living their lives, online and offline, solely based on trying to satisfy, not people, but hashtags, simple words that have suddenly skyrocketed to fame just because a handful of trolls on the Internet deemed them "cool," "popular," and "in."

We dedicate more time researching the best hashtags and key phrases to post than we do for research papers and class assignments. We schedule our days around the "best times" to post images on the popular app so we can "try to gain the most likes and followers." We deliberately take photos from different and unconventional angles so we have "something" to brag about, even if we don't stand by what we say, and even if we know our photos are doctored.

As human beings living in the contemporary civilization that is social media, we rely on any means we find possible to make ourselves seem more alluring and more well-rounded to the outside world. We deceive ourselves into believing that we are actually living our lives to the fullest, when in reality, we take stock photo-worthy images of a bowl of fruit sitting on our coffee tables with the caption, "Just moved into my new place by the beach in Miami!" #livingitup #beachlife4ever, when in truth, we have gone nowhere.

#obsessed
Instagram Exposes Humanity

We experience mental breakdowns when our smartphones die before we get the chance to post selfies of ourselves with captions about how bored we are at work...instead of actually working. We purposefully dress ourselves up with makeup and new outfit purchases just so we have something new and different we can boast about. We spend hours learning how to use Lightroom and Photoshop just so we can alter our seemingly dull images into images that can potentially receive millions of likes and comments.

We try so hard to become someone, to become one of the many influencers on the Internet who may or may not be Internet bots, that we fail to realize how much we have become addicted to our Instagram lives, so dependent that we have even resorted to means beyond simple Photoshopping to get the followers we want; we have resorted to buying fake likes and fake followers.

"Local Woman Becomes Bankrupt for Temporary Fame."

"Instagram Fraud: Is Anything She Posts Real Anymore?"

"Travel Blogger Fools Public with Green Screen Backdrops."

"InstaFame or InstaFake?"

In today's society, the world of social media has become an addictive drug, a compulsion that does not discriminate by demographics. Originally cultivated as a simple mean of communication with friends and lost acquaintances, social media platforms such as Facebook and Instagram have opened gates for obsession and abuse. We hide behind our screens when we are too afraid to mock or torment others to their faces.

We block friends and lovers way too impulsively because we allow our personal feelings and strong desire for attention to overpower our connections. We give up friendships and relationships because we misinterpret Internet images and messages as personal attacks, or we become so focused on achieving a few seconds of fame that we expose our secrets and hurt those we love.

"Hangin' at the club with some hot new babes.
Girlfriend ain't got no strings on me." #freedom
#bachelorlife #infidelity

Since the rise of Instagram, other popular social sharing platforms, such as Facebook and Twitter, have declined significantly, with a 17% decrease in Facebook usage among American youth and young adults, from 79% to 62%, while the use of Instagram has increased from 64% to 66%.

The rise of social media, smartphones, and text messaging has driven families and soulful interactions apart, where young and once-naïve children can now be seen scrolling through Instagram feeds at the dinner table, where dating is left out in the cold when couples care more about the "perfect selfie" or "foodie shot" to post than the dates themselves, and where groups of friends sitting at the same table are seen texting each other.

We have become so alienated from one another that it almost becomes abnormal to make a phone call or to not use social media, becoming more attached to devices and virtual worlds than people we are with. We have become so disconnected from those right in front of us and the environment that surrounds us that we seek validation for connection elsewhere, aka, the Internet.

What happens when social media falls, coming to an inevitable end? What happens when our Internet lives are no longer recognized, or when we no longer have a sharing platform we can use to brag about our lives? What happens when that selfie we take is just an image that stays on our phones? What happens when we no longer have a horde of followers lusting over our travel and food images?

Will we still enjoy these hobbies we claim to enjoy? Will our lives still remain the same even when we no longer have an outlet to boast about our accomplishments? Will we still feel a purpose and drive to continue our lifestyles even when no one is around to see them? Or will we lose that motivation completely and admit that we only live the lives we claim to live for the attention of the those whom we do not even know?

Detrimental Clout of Social Media

"You mean nothing!"

"Your life is trash. You should really accomplish more with your life."

"Your feed is nothing compared to hers. She has five times the followers and ten times the likes that you do. You're nothing. You shouldn't even be on social media."

18

#obsessed
Instagram Exposes Humanity

"Everything you've done is pathetic. You don't know the first thing about traveling and, yet, you try to pride yourself on it."

"Get off the Internet. You're never going to amount to anything."

"If you don't visit 100 countries within the next year, you're done."

"You're a loser. Figure out a new hobby."

"Dude, you bought followers. Does your page even mean anything? How many of them are actually real?"

"Why are you catering to a bunch of bots? Do you realize how ridiculous that is? Wasting all that money just to showcase dumb pictures to a bunch of dumb robots? You're an idiot!"

"You better post a new country on your page every week. Otherwise, your page is useless!"

"Do you even like traveling? Are you only traveling so you can put it on Instagram?"

"Your pictures are terrible! You are never going to match up to the fame of others because your filters suck!"

"You need to learn Photoshop if you want to be #instafamous. Otherwise, you're a piece of shit."

"Are you even enjoying what you do, or is it all for show?"

"Are you even traveling for yourself, or so you can show others your life doesn't suck?"

"Are you even happy?"

Trolling and cyberbullying affect over 90% of users on social networks, especially in college populations, and with over 50% of those populations resorting to successful suicides due to their social media obsessions, social media proves more deadly than alcohol and drug addictions combined.

The simple action of scrolling a finger up and down a phone can transform from a short five minutes of leisure activity into entire days wasted. People spend hours upon hours every day scrolling through posts from feeds of their fellow Instagram icons, aweing in vain over a life they wish they could possess while spending their remaining hours trying to concoct their own lavish posts, spending more time on their phones than on every other aspect of their lives.

Students neglect their studies and class assignments to take selfies in attempts to generate the most likes, as well as deprive themselves of sleep and nutrition as their focuses become consumed by the number of hearts they receive. Employees spend over half their time at work on their phones, taking multiple breaks throughout their days to scroll through feeds, neglecting their responsibilities both at work and in their homes.

"When people spend hours liking photos and creating the 'perfect post' but still do not see what they had hoped for in return, and they usually don't, depression and anxiety set in hard, and the addiction persists."

However, a lack of self-control is not to blame when it comes to Instagram addiction. These social sharing platforms are intentionally designed to become addictive so companies can channel optimal usage of their platforms for increased profit.

Addiction to social media can become just as intense as addiction to heroine or alcohol. People can spend years hooked on something, whatever that something may be, that releases satisfaction into their brains, experiencing withdrawal symptoms such as extreme anxiety and feral anger when they try to step away, and throwing away their integrities and authentic lives for falsified ones in order to gain superficial approval.

"Cases of cyberbullying have risen drastically over the past decade with the increase in social media opportunities. The revolution of online correspondences has cultivated physical and mental damages to individuals all around the world, defined by online associations and advances that cause risks to secure and mental prosperities, and proven to employ life-long damages on those of all stages of life, especially young adults."

Victims of Internet cyberbullying have been known to experience critical antagonisms such as peer pressure, depression, substance abuse, eating disorders, and a reduced quality of ethics. It has become so dangerous that we find it difficult to distinguish between actual danger and perceived danger as we become disconnected from reality and begin to see the lives we have falsified as truths.

#obsessed
Instagram Exposes Humanity

In 2019, a Canadian investigator conducted a research study with a sample size of 188 female college undergraduates and found that those who engaged in virtual comparisons of themselves with the broader population of females, real or Photoshop-constructed, dramatically decreased their self-esteems and self-perceived appearances when associated with those they felt were much more attractive. However, the negative consequences of these side-by-side comparisons don't just stop there.

A study published in 2018 in the Journal of Social and Clinical Psychology showed that quality of life and overall performance in daily activities significantly decreased with increased and unlimited use of social networks including, but not limited to, Facebook, Snapchat, and Instagram.

Online pressure and abuse increase nervousness and melancholy in individuals, youth especially, who constantly worry about trying to fit in and becoming well-liked and accepted by their peers, resorting to any means possible to achieve these goals regardless of whether they fall through the cracks and destroy themselves.

The more their likeability feels threatened, the more they feel the need to become attached to their phones and social media pages, without stopping until they feel secure enough to step away for even a few minutes, and never putting themselves in the position where they do not have 24/7 access to the Internet.

However, those individuals who scroll through their Instagram feeds late at night are the ones most vulnerable to the negative effects of the social media population, bringing out more trolls and deception as people become more sensitive to identity crises. This causes them to become more sleep-deprived with less motivation for other life responsibilities, channeling all their focus onto misinterpreting and envying that of which they see on their online networks. As a result, the feeling of helplessness and discouragement surge as they feel imprisoned by the words of those they don't even know or the images of those they want but cannot have, triggering their emotional reactions as opposed to their rational selves.

Research has also found that social media addiction provides a direct and positive correlation with stress and stress-related consequences, including dejection, negative body perception, and poor self-esteem, especially for young adults, late teens, and the female population, in which they respond by lashing out against their loved ones, seeking undeserved revenge in response to what they see on the Internet, and engaging in poor choices such as self-starvation and drug abuse in attempts to give their "followers" what they want or to become better "influencers" for certain crowds, creating an age where life choices are based upon the decisions made by the selfish desires of strangers.

Although social media was intentionally designed to help human beings stay connected to loved ones, colleagues, acquaintances, and missed connections, it has unintentionally also driven them apart, instigating constant competition and animosity against those who don't relish in their posts or against those who criticize images of others for their own attempted attention-seeking behaviors. Rates of kidnapping and murder have also been on the rise as individuals become so desperate to generate more followers that they fall for scams of "guaranteed likes" or fake photoshoots for "perfect Instagram pictures."

Deadly Wrath of Hashtags

#gym. #summer. #workout. #autumn. #model. #instapic. #happiness. #motivation. #life. #cool. #hot. #music. #hair. #instamood. #beauty. #landscape. #repost. #ootd. #photography. #inspiration.

"Instagram is a drug, a digital drug, with an abuse of hashtags used to push our posts up the superficial ladder for all to pretend to admire. Hashtags are going to kill our generation."

#obsessed
Instagram Exposes Humanity

Less than two decades ago, the word "hashtag" was not even in existence. The symbol "#" used to resemble the "pound key" on telephones but has now exploded into a symbol of representation and belonging. We cannot speak a simple phrase or write a simple post without the word "hashtag" spilling out of our mouths or through the tips of our fingers.

We feel the need to #hashtag every word we deem popular, and we sometimes even go as far as to make up words that don't even exist just so we can hashtag them. We waste hours scouring the Internet for the "most popular hashtags" or the "most commonly used hashtags" to enhance our profiles so we can portray ourselves as the best we can be.

We stalk "influencers" we admire and believe have millions of followers so we can steal their hashtags and gain the number of likes they receive. We fail to limit ourselves to just a few relevant hashtags because we possess the mentality that "more is better," and we end up falling into the trap of #overkill when we saturate our meaningful posts with hashtags we cannot even stand by because we use them more as competition than as personal labels.

Unfortunately, without hashtags, Instagram posts inevitably become lost in the midst, difficult to discover in a saturated environment where everyone strives to be someone. Our feeds and profile pages can only be known and potentially liked if we throw popular hashtags onto them; otherwise, we end up in a perpetual state of no likes nor followers. Even so, creating the "perfect" Instagram post has proven to be a difficult task for ordinary people who aren't celebrities.

#obsessed
Instagram Exposes Humanity

Despite positioning at certain angles, polishing photos with the best filters, and coming up with creative and eye-catching captions, grabbing hold of the greatest hashtags can either make or break Instagram posts. It doesn't matter if we pour our emotional hearts out into our posts or if we take an image that represents a stock photo; if we don't slap on a #metoo, our posts are considered #nothing. Someone who writes an essay on rescuing dolphins, with over ten humanitarian photos, can receive the same exact number of likes as someone who takes a selfie and throws on #selfie beneath it, an unfortunate truth that many Instagram users feel destroy the authenticity of social-sharing platforms.

Rise of Instagram to Notoriety

Launched in 2010 as a photo-sharing application with a meagre 25,000 users, Instagram has taken over the social media world throughout the past several years. Unlike former social media hosts like Myspace and Facebook, Instagram requires minimal effort to show the world our "fantastic" lives, lives as popular as those seen on reality television shows. Instagram takes away the work and effort of having to construct long and interesting stories so people will stop their scrolling and pause for a moment on our pages.

Instagram allows us to spend less than a minute on an image, where writing one simple sentence or hashtag can cause hundreds of likes to flock toward us. We are creatures who base what we like on what we encounter visually. We see Instagram as photo-pornography and find it way too easy to simply tap on a couple of images we find interesting and feed the egos of those who post them.

"As the demand for social media platforms increase, those who can accomplish ways to give users the most reward for the least amount of work have become the superpowers of the world, creating more addicting ways to get gullible zombies to create accounts so they can continue their rise to the top, fully aware that they are ruining traditional human-to-human interactions of our once-civilized society."

Nowadays, it's considered a "sin" to not have at least one social media account, whether it is Facebook, Twitter, Snapchat, YouTube, or Instagram, and if you have all five, then you are seen as someone who deserves to recognized and known, or so that's what we like to believe. The more social media accounts we have, the more we are seen as too desperate to fit in and trying too hard to portray a life that does not exist.

Having a million followers on the Internet, 99.9% of whom we don't even know, does not make us important and deserving of attention. Becoming an "Internet sensation" for mocking the elderly does not make our lives more worth living than the lives of others. Who cares how many likes we get per post?

Most of the people who like our posts are only randomly clicking on our images to get likes back, not because they actually believe our posts are magnificent.

Who cares if our follower count shoots up by twice as much in one day? What's the point of having thousands upon thousands of followers when we end up alone after putting down our phones?

Social sharing networks like Instagram have boosted our egos to unimaginable levels, and not in a positive way. We shame ourselves and others when theirs or our profiles don't look pristine, and we base our self-worth and importance by how many comments we receive on a daily basis.

We secretly (and sometimes, openly) judge others and demean them when they only receive two likes while we have received five, using these numbers as a measure of self-worth. We become so fame-hungry for virtual popularity that we forget how to be human, and we treat other human beings with disrespect and hatred just to climb that ladder of temptation to...nowhere.

Don't get me started on how we treat those who are NOT on social media. We see Instagram accounts as sacred rites of passage to life, and when we hear of people who don't have one, we either peer pressure them by making their current lives feel worthless otherwise, or we ignore them completely to avoid being associated with "unpopular" individuals, caring more about having a colony of followers online than a colony of followers in real life. When we are at the brink of death and ready to give up, who will be there to pull us off from the edge of the bridge? Our colony of Instagram followers commenting on our suicidal posts for us to step off rather than actually pulling us off?

"Your nose looks fake. I bet you had plastic surgery. You're a fake!"

"No wonder you're still single. Your face is too big, and you're too short!"

"How dare you wear a shirt supporting that company? You're a sell-out!"

"Ew! What the fuck are you wearing?! That's a fashion-don't!"

"I hate your face! I bet you don't have any friends. You're a loser. You suck!"

"Your voice makes me want to burn my ears. Get off the Internet!"

Instagram makes us ignore and reject those we used to call "friends" and "family," breaking up with our partners because the Internet does not approve or blocking our parents because we think they embarrass us. We isolate people we used to love in real life because the virtual world manipulates us into doing so rather than of our own choosing. We see close friends as scarred and flawed because we have tried so hard to fit in with the popular crowd that we would rather risk losing childhood friends than risk becoming isolated ourselves for having our own opinions and for standing our grounds.

We make decisions influenced by others that we later on regret...when it becomes too late. It no longer matters how long we have known people; one mistake or one misspoken word can cause us to banish and ghost those we care about, even when we don't understand why we are doing so. We no longer give people chances to redeem themselves because we have been trained to screen out those who don't meet specific criteria. We have been taught to only befriend those within the inner circle of popularity if we want to remain "popular," "well-liked," and "on top."

"Instagram is like a high school cafeteria. We sit with those who can boost our popularity, admiring the 'influencers' from a near distance, hoping to one day get the chance to sit with them. Sitting with those who are considered 'losers' will only warrant harassment, and if we do not belong in any group, we may as well eat in a toilet stall."

The problem with social media is that we find it that much easier to unleash our criticism and negativity online because we're not forced to come face-to-face with those we mock and put down. Before the world of the Internet, we filter our strong opinions, fearing shame or anger from those we taunt.

However, when we have that chance to hide behind a screen like cowards, we become deadly and extreme, tossing every insult and every criticism out in the open rather than holding the hurtful ones in. We pick fights with everyone, despite who they are, when we get to remain anonymous in the process. We say things we would never have the nerves to say otherwise, and we dispute back and forth even after we have driven individuals to their own suicides, refusing to stop until we meet our very own deaths.

If we take the time and stop to think about it, rather than taking selfies in the middle of a highway, scrolling through people's profiles and feeds is just a modern way of stalking them. The word "following" means what it always meant, despite whether it's over the Internet. We are literally spending our days and nights stalking other people online and trying too hard to be like them. It's insane! We are like the crazy serial killers we see in movies, where the psychopaths are obsessed with their prey. The only difference is, we don't resort to killing those we stalk, not most of us anyway.

But, instead, we try to copy and be like those we admire, generating account names, image profiles, captions, and filters similar to those who generate the most likes in attempts to also generate the same amounts of likes. It's not as diabolical as serially-killing people, but it's not something we should be proud of either. We follow Instagram "influencers" so much that we end up knowing more about their lives than we do our own.

We follow their every move and force ourselves to behave like them, including eating the same food, dressing in the same clothes, and even speaking the same as them despite it being clearly fake. We become incrementally obsessed with complete strangers that our initial intentions of joining Instagram, whether socially, as a brand, or as a business, become lost because we give up our individualities to chase after "what's in" just because we believe changing ourselves will make us more well-liked. And if that's not bad enough, we sometimes even become envious of "Instagram pet influencers." How low have our lives sunk when we become less popular than a pig in a tutu?

"We judge others by their looks, their height, their skin color, their size, their age, their ethnicities, and their personal life choices when, secretly, we wish others would stop judging us based on our own."

"We criticize web-based profiles based on what we see rather than what we know, and we showcase our own profiles based on who we want to be rather than who we actually are."

"We put others down again and again over the Internet, pulling down their self-esteems, until they no longer have the motivation to continue and are forced to drop off the world of social media."

"We determine who we like and dislike based on how others on the Internet foolishly influence us, and we become miserable later in life when we regret having made decisions outside of our own choosing."

"We hate ourselves because the Internet tells us we are not worthy of life."

Instagram Against the Test of Time

Instagram. Facebook. YouTube. When it comes to social media platforms, what do we usually associate with happiness and success? Likes! We let our worth be determined by how many people approve of us on a daily basis, and when we receive a negative comment, we allow our lives to become destroyed by it.

However, what is it that makes Instagram stand out amongst these other social platforms, rising to the top at an exponential rate? The answer: feasibility and limited work. Even though we continue to base our lives on the approval of others on all social platforms, unlike Facebook and YouTube, both of which require more effort than just a simple picture, Instagram makes it easy to replace a single photo or a simple hashtag when they don't get approved. When we don't get enough hearts on an Instagram photo, we have no problem getting rid of it and slapping on a new one in its place. YouTube, on the other hand, is much more difficult to just delete and re-post because a lot of effort and time have gone into perfecting that video.

With Instagram photos, millions of people take 100 images of the same item or the same selfie at once, coating each one with a different filter with the intention of posting at least 40% of those images per day as each one fails to generate the expected number of likes. When that fails to go as planned, we enter a phase known as "Insta-pulse," where after scrolling through the endless photos we have on our phones and STILL failing to find one that works, we end up posting a mediocre image in its place because we believe that posting a shitty image is better than nothing at all because it shows that we are still actively present online and, therefore, alive.

For those of us desperate enough, we create five different accounts to increase our odds of becoming an influencer, one for our "fashion sense," one for our "foodie recipes," one for our "whimsical travels," one for our "desired musical talents," and one for our "selfie wall of shame." "One of them has got to be a winner," we tell ourselves as we lose motivation to continue posting onto any of them after two months of not getting the likes we expected.

#obsessed
Instagram Exposes Humanity

"Immediate gratification is a bitch to our patience."

"Our captions can also make or break our posts, but let's face it, we all know originality means nothing as people tend to vote for overused motivational quotes and sappy song lyrics."

Instagram began as a social platform for connections and happiness through accomplishments and images others share. However, as the popularity increased, so did the competition as people began to sought after each other's profiles for the sake of getting tips or getting others to feature them on their profiles rather than seeking true connections.

We also tear down those we actually admire because, one, our comments on the photos of top influencers will definitely get us noticed and, two, we put our envy and jealousy on our plates and despise those who seem to be doing better than us with minimal to no effort.

Instagram allows for #like4like or #comment4comment because of its competitive nature. We falsely believe that if we spend 10 hours a day liking photos of others, then they will like our photos back, or we believe that following a bunch of people with the hashtag #follow4follow will get them to follow us back, and they do, for about a day or two, until they decide not to, exemplifying one of the most common scams in the book to generate followers without having to follow nonsense and irrelevant accounts.

More dangerously, Instagram's photo- and video-sharing features, plus their live feed opportunity, tempt users to take ridiculous selfies and narrate life stories of what they eat during every meal or describe their daily outfits WHILE they are driving to work or taking an exam. The live feed feature makes us feel the need to make EVERY PART of our lives live, whether people care about what we put out there or not.

Since the release of Instagram highlights, we have the people who post 1-2 highlights per week while the majority of us post 1-2 highlights per minute, telling entire stories about nothing on our highlights, whining about our days on our highlights, or filling our highlights with excessive photos we have left over from choosing our "best ones" to post.

Whenever we get a manicure, a new hairstyle, a new nose, or a new makeover, we can't help but overwhelm our profiles and boast about it, taking "flawless selfies" from every angle until we finally get one that knocks people off their feet. Similar to Internet stars and celebrities who are obsessed with posting new selfies of themselves daily, we try too hard to become noticed as we foolishly believe that selfies in vain and perfect external appearances are the only ways to achieve fame.

"Wealthier" IG users feel the need to showcase their lavish materialism despite whether they're living in debt, posting images of themselves in designer clothing, holding designer handbags such as Louis Vuitton or Prada with #fab or #lux while demeaning their followers as poor "peasants" when they can't also upload images of thousands of dollars in cash (which, by the way, is a stupid way to get targeted and burglarized). They find themselves living through social media, living via a constructed app that has inhibited their abilities to live in the present moment.

#obsessed
Instagram Exposes Humanity

"We can travel to beautiful mountains in foreign countries and still only remain focused on our selfies and the perfect filters to post rather than the sceneries themselves."

"We can see beautiful sunsets but still choose to watch them through our screens rather than through our naked eyes. I once experienced a magnificent sunset over clear waters on a beach in Cape May, NJ, and over 90% of the people there whipped out their phones to videotape it instead of enjoying the moment."

"It's sickening how we cannot enjoy simple moments without feeling the need to share them with others as well."

"It's as if we think that unless we have proof of our travels or proof of the beauty we see, others will not believe that we have actually seen them. Who the fuck cares?"

"We do not need to prove ourselves to others. So, what if people don't believe that we have been to Antarctica? Those with proof are usually those seeking attention or those with Photoshopped images."

"Stop living for the approval of others."

When I had a semi-successful Instagram travel account of 20,000 followers, a micro-influencer account as people like to call it, I would always get messages and comments on places I SHOULD be visiting, allowing those comments to drive where I traveled to rather than visiting places I WANTED to go. I always felt the pressure to visit certain countries, wasting money on destinations I didn't really want to see just so I could hang onto my followers, and when I didn't have the time to visit these places, I saw my follower count drop off one by one when I failed to share new images. I saw my love for traveling slowly diminish as I struggled to keep up with the constant demand, and I began to question who I was traveling for.

Instagram users love consistency. Unless we're posting beautiful and flawless images every day of unique surroundings with savvy captions, we might as well see our IG lives fall through the cracks. People will begin to dislike us and find us as no longer worth following unless we can give them what they want all the time. It's no wonder being an Instagram influencer is a full-time job.

For those of us who are unfortunate enough to work 9-5 jobs without the freedom to spend six hours on a simple post, we struggle to keep our social lives intact. Not all of us can travel to a different country every week or dress in a new outfit every day. Unless our entire focus 24/7 is solely on Instagram, we're bound to lose followers, followers that take twice as much effort to gain back, followers we don't even know.

This competitive world makes us ignore memories and stories that make us unique. We lose confidence in ourselves and forget the past experiences that made us different and special. We see our ups and downs in life as flaws rather than as lessons. We see our personal preferences as damaging rather than as special to ourselves, constructing profile pictures based on feedback from critics than based on who we truly are.

Instagram's Triumph Over Facebook

Facebook once ruled the social media world. The idea of allowing people to connect with those from same schools based on mutual friends and to find missed and lost connections (while also stalking exes and crushes left and right) provided the opportunity to truly judge a book by its cover and uphold the standards of society in order to be liked and in order to isolate others who just do not match up to the caliber.

Instagram, on the other hand, allows us to become Internet sensations by flashing our smiles and our asses without needing to be intelligent or speaking a single word. It has taken us decades back to a time where women should be seen and not heard, making humanity look shallow and superfluous.

However, for some odd reason and destroying what we have fought for all these years, Instagram's popularity continues to rise, with over 300 million users compared to the 228 million users on Facebook. Plus, we all know that when we're stalking others, all we care about are their photos and whether we look better than them.

Another reason why Instagram has taken over the reign that was Facebook is the false feeling of power by having "worshippers," aka "followers." Facebook's main connection is with friends, i.e., adding friends, blocking friends, poking friends, etc.

On the flip side, Instagram refers to these "friends" as "followers," where people follow each other like hungry dogs in heat, and so it's natural that the more "followers" people have, the more likely they are to believe they're royalty. The live feature and story highlights that Instagram offer also allow people to showcase their lives 24/7 with false beliefs that their "followers" are just sitting on their couches at home, pawning over the lives they wish they could have and envious of those they follow.

Instagram allows us to avoid the trouble of scrolling through feeds, where we can just click on several story highlights at once and see years' worth of life stories in a time span of 10 minutes.

"The use of social media has skyrocketed over the past decade."

"In 2005, only 5% of adults in the United States reported using a social media platform, whereas now, that number has increased to over 70%, higher among the younger population, with over 81% having some sort of social media life, paired with a continual decrease in intellectual knowledge and mental prosperity."

"Over 13% of adolescents reported being cyberbullied at least once in their online lives, and over 60% self-reported as being either supremacists, misogynists, or homophobes."

The Internet allows us to be anything and anybody we want that would otherwise be looked down on in real life. We have teenage boys presenting themselves as drag queens. We have middle-aged men presenting themselves as makeup artists. We have ordinary people presenting themselves as celebrities. We all hate the idea of catfishing but only because we hate being the victims of catfishing.

We live in a world where we feel forced to catfish in order to fit into this constantly moving civilization. We also date and flirt more often online than we ever have in real life. Exposing ourselves and becoming vulnerable to others online are much easier because that anxiety and that fear of rejection become relinquished. We handle rejection with more composure when we don't have to deal with those rejecting us face-to-face. We even have sex online, sending dick pics and nudes to more strangers than we do our own partners.

#obsessed
Instagram Exposes Humanity

How did Instagram allow people to become so fake and so phony? As the app has developed, so has the weight of the world on people's shoulders to construct amazing profiles or risk becoming social outcasts. There are rules to posting on social media; it's no longer a relaxing activity to enjoy with loved ones.

These unwritten rules include how we can't post excessively, that the images we do share must be absolutely perfect regardless of what the photos are of, and we must post every single day even if we aren't in the mood or don't have the content. Authenticity has deteriorated as a result of this because most people online no longer represent who they are in real life.

"Who's to blame for this downward progression from authenticity to triviality?"

"Have societal standards become so high that we need to pretend to become what's socially acceptable in order to be socially accepted, or have the images of ourselves become so flawed that we can never be happy with who we are?"

"Why is it that we have become obsessed with creating accounts that represent those of privileged and famous people, continuing to fall into the trap of lavish lifestyles even when we know they're all fake?"

"We would rather be known as 'potential wannabes', 'social jokes', and 'sellouts' than not be known as anyone at all because negative attention is still attention. And you know how we play off and excuse negative attention? #haters!"

#obsessed
Instagram Exposes Humanity

In the midst of fake photographs and accounts created by bots, the rise of "Finstagram" or "Finsta" has risen into popularity, otherwise known as phony Instagram. Finsta is especially popular among the younger generations as it has taken our desires to portray fake profiles and given us the opportunity and reason to create fake accounts.

We look at Finsta and think it's such a far-fetched and ridiculous idea to spend time constructing profiles that don't even represent the true persons, but at the same time, that's exactly what we do every day on Instagram when we filter and alter our images; we're just too oblivious and ignorant to realize and accept that our online profiles are all fake.

Although most people use Finstagram to troll others and post images of their "ugly" selves, which are most often truly unfiltered images, it's these same behaviors that make this version of Instagram that much more authentic than the actual version of Instagram. With Finsta, people don't need to hide behind a beauty shell nor hold back and refrain themselves from speaking their minds like we often do for Instagram to avoid being judged. With Finsta, it's okay letting our authentic selves be free.

Obsession with the Instagram Profile

Our Instagram profiles make or break our Instagram lives. In order to have any sort of social life or following, our profile names need to be on point, our images need to be pristine, and we need to post like we are people with captions worthy of being read. That means, we need to force ourselves to dedicate hours per image, per post, in order to receive any sort of attention, with the exact hashtags pasted at the end to really make our photos shine.

We start off with a certain message we want to portray or even just a few simple pictures we want to show so we can communicate with those close to us. However, somewhere between the midst of feeling like a loser and wanting to get noticed, we become the wannabes we mock in the first place, resorting to the same behaviors we swore to ourselves we never would.

How many Instagram profiles online are genuine compared to just masks? How many of the "influencers" we see are true influencers as opposed to bots or frauds? The problem is, we can't tell. We tear down those who are actually authentic, with real people trying their best to showcase their best selves, and we resonate on emotional levels with those who will never respond to or recognize us because they literally can't. We see what we want to see and ignore the signs telling us that those we seek to be are not even human beings.

However, it's not our faults for being so obsessed with seeking the perfect profiles. Subpar profiles are damaging and can present just as dangerous to our social lives. We're almost forced to manipulate our profiles in order to stay afloat. Otherwise, we might as well just give up Instagram forever. Bland-looking profiles are useless when it comes to the Instagram world because Instagram is all about pleasuring the eyes. Images that are dull and dark are less likely to grab the attention of potential likes while images that generate a theme with glamorous filters are more likely to attract followers.

If you Google "Instagram filters," you will see "influencers" and "wannabe influencers" selling filters left and right, and people jump over hoops to buy them because they believe "perfect filters" are key to millions of followers despite what is being advertised. In the Instagram world, a profile with 500 selfies adorned with perfect filters of luminescent rainbow colors becomes more popular than a profile with 500 unfiltered images of world travels.

But do we realize how desperate we all are to attract the attention of strangers, spending our hard-earned salaries on filters and outfits to please the eyes of people we don't even know? What people want is changing daily. The hilarious Internet cat that receives 10,000 likes in one day can barely achieve 5 likes a week later. Pink filters that were "all the rage" last month can become hated the next month. It's extremely difficult keeping up with the social media world because it's constantly shifting.

Those who are able to stand by their messages and their goals despite the changing world are the ones truly happy and proud of what they do. For the majority of us, we move with the changing world, jumping from fashion to food to travel to music to animals, unsure of which direction we want to turn our images toward and creating new profile after new profile to ensure that one of these profiles will showcase the themes we believe are "in."

We can't satisfy everyone on the Internet. There will always be critics despite how great our images look or how beautiful our filters are. We see fashion bloggers steering from couture and luxury outfits #ootd to food vloggers in front of iPhone cameras. We see foodies steering from #bestfoodever at hidden local treasures to selfies in front of Photoshopped screens of Paris. At the end of the day, who are we really trying to impress?

#obsessed
Instagram Exposes Humanity

"Instagram influencers post images of themselves licking toilet seats and street lamps. How low do they have to stoop before we realize they're not worth following?"

Reality Versus Delusion

When we first created that coveted Instagram profile, many of us saw it as a fun opportunity to showcase our best selves and share our special moments with our friends and family.

However, somewhere down the line, we began getting addicted to it, thinking we are using this social media platform for ourselves, when in reality, we have turned into using it to make sure the world knows that we are better than others based on how many likes and followers we can collect, a way to boost our egos and show off to others that we have what they do not.

Needless to say, Instagram is a psychological mind-fuck that makes the majority of us hate ourselves. Despite being "loved" by millions of kids and adults around the world, this photograph-based platform is also a venue for elevated levels of anxiety, stress, depression, harassments, abuse, FOMO (fear of missing out), self-hatred for not measuring up, and dread for living lives seen as less significant than lives of others.

Of the major social media platforms we have all come to love, YouTube ranks the highest for promoting the well-being and prosperity of its users, with Twitter and Facebook trailing behind as second and third, respectively, followed by Snapchat and Instagram as dead last.

When we think about what we actually accomplish on Instagram, what are the first things that usually pop into our minds? We THINK we use Instagram in ways we are meant to on this platform, posting images, liking pictures of our friends and family members, commenting on posts and responding to posts on our own feeds, and sharing our major highlights with others so they can relish in our celebrations.

However, how we ACTUALLY use Instagram is a little different. After taking 1,000 images on one single trip or event, we spend days sorting through the best ones and choosing the best filters for them as natural lighting is just not good enough. We then post these images with witty captions that we either steal from others or off the

Internet and pray that our one post will blow up with likes within the next hour. When that fails to happen, we remove that picture and repeat the process five more times before we finally either give up or run out of "good" pictures to showcase.

Next, we obsessively stalk other profiles and find the ones with the highest following counts, and like a lunatic, we like 30 images in a row of theirs so they will be forced to recognize us and check out our profiles in return. As we all know, one like or one comment from a top influencer automatically drives their followers to our accounts, and when that happens, our power begins to rise.

However, when that doesn't happen, we continue to obsessively stalk profiles of influencers and even non-influencers in attempts to generate some likes back. #like4like. And when that also fails, we pull out the vicious and manipulative tactics by criticizing images of influencers in attempts to start a controversial war that will indeed get us noticed.

After all, if an influencer posts an image with a perfect backdrop of Mount Everest while also wearing a sundress, we can't help but call them out as being fake; we're only saying what everyone else is afraid to say. We use Instagram as if it is our own personal game of cat and mouse, chasing after the one goal that everyone has of becoming a verified influencer and refusing to let anything get in our ways of achieving that goal. We allow our jealous and competitive natures to force us to tear down innocent people just because we hate that we are not them, and we destroy ourselves night after night for not being able to be them despite how much effort we put in.

Instagram's web-based photo option that's supposed to represent "real life" (but really doesn't) causes us to have unreasonable and unrealistic desires to reach for stars we cannot possibly grasp, creating low confidence and ineptness in ourselves. We see an image of an Instagram influencer prancing in front of an uncrowded Taj Mahal during peak season with #unfiltered, driving up our own anticipation for that same chance to also see the uncrowded iconic monument during peak season.

However, thousands of dollars and 20 hours on a plane later, we come to realize that this "unfiltered" image doesn't actually exist as we become surrounded by thousands of other eager tourists hoping to catch a solo selfie with the monument as they have also been fooled by Instagrammers, regretting their trips as they are now lost in a city with a language they cannot speak nor understand.

For about half of us, we're logical enough to realize that we have been tricked by photo manipulations or green screens. We're smart enough to not be fooled again by an image of the Great Wall of China or Times Square in New York City with barely any people, an image "influencers" just ripped off from Google. However, for the other half of us, we take this personally.

Despite the impossibilities, we still believe these photos are real and that the reason we cannot accomplish the same photos is because we have either arrived at the wrong time, that we are just unlucky, that we just suck at taking pictures, or that we just suck in general. Despite all the red flags pointing to fake Instagram pictures, such as the same cloud in every image, a pink hue over every photo that doesn't actually exist in reality, or the fact that there are no people at the most popular tourist sites, some people still choose to believe that their "influencer idols" are 100% authentic and still strive to become like them, as impossible as it is to do so, and as a result, we become demotivated to continue on as we realize we can never measure up to the photography skills of "the best."

"Instagram causes young men and women to hate the way their bodies look because they cannot Photoshop their mirrors."

"Instagram makes individuals feel like their lives are not worth living because they do not exude a glow of purple and blue hue."

"Instagram makes us feel pressured to do more and more even when we don't want to or else we're left feeling terrible about ourselves.

"Instagram makes us want to kill ourselves because our best always warrants negative comments from others, and trying to accommodate our critics will always warrant negative comments from ourselves."

And when that isn't enough, we resort to breaking the rules to drive our Instagram popularity up despite what it takes. We utilize banned hashtags, such as #adulting, #dating, and #fuck, at the risk of getting our accounts banned because we believe that using these hashtags will help us stand out and drive others toward our profiles. We will do anything to generate comments on our posts, whether positive or negative, because being the most controversial person on the Internet beats being a nobody.

#alone. #always. #armparty. #adulting. #assday. #ass.
#assworship. #asiangirl. #beautyblogger. #brain. #boho.
#besties. #bikinibody. #costumes. #curvygirls. #date.
#dating. #desk. #dm. #direct. #elevator. #eggplant.
#edm. #fuck. #girlsonly. #gloves. #graffitiigers.
#happythanksgiving. #hawks. #hotweather. #humpday.
#hustler. #ilovemyinstagram. #instababy. #instasport.
#iphonegraphy. #italiano. #ice. #killingit. #kansas.
#kissing. #kickoff. #leaves. #like. #lulu. #lean. #master.
#milf. #mileycyrus. #models. #mustfollow. #nasty.
#newyearsday. #nude. #nudism. #nudity. #overnight.
#orderweedonline. #parties. #petite. #pornfood.
#pushups. #prettygirl. #rate. #ravens. #samelove.
#selfharm. #skateboarding. #skype. #snap. #snapchat.
#single. #singlelife. #stranger. #saltwater. #shower.
#shit. #sopretty. #sunbathing. #streetphoto. #swole.
#snowstorm. #sun. #sexy. #tanlines. #todayimwearing.
#teens. #teen. #thought. #tag4like. #tagsforlikes.
#thighs. #undies. #valentinesday. #workflow. #wtf.
#xanax. #youngmodel.

Many of us also turn to using robots in attempts to boost
our profiles, from buying fake likes and followers (which
will be touched upon more later) to deceitfully enhancing
our popularity or utilizing software and apps that auto-
like or auto-follow similar profiles to ours based on a few
key hashtags. These bots are designed by companies to
perform what humans generally do on Instagram,
following/unfollowing and liking/unliking, but at an
exponential rate, liking random images and randomly
posting nonsense comments on users' profiles that don't
add any value or sense.

Since one of the oldest tactics in the book for gaining
more followers is to follow users, wait for them to follow

back, and then unfollow them, bots are also designed to do this, but again, at an expedited rate, causing Instagram to catch onto this scheme and block accounts who are seen liking, commenting, and following at a rate more than the average human is able to do. However, despite accounts being blocked, we continue to do this anyway, waiting for our accounts to become unblocked and then repeating the process all over, until we are either banned completely, or we realize the truth that the results generated from these bots are only temporary, lasting for a month or two and then disappearing, causing us to lose both our money and our self-dignities.

#repost or #regram is another tactic that many IG users use to get their accounts noticed by others. Similar to #retweets, as seen on Twitter, where people see a tweet from someone else they find interesting or worthy of sharing and re-tweet it on their own accounts, allowing others to indirectly associate them with said brilliant tweet. Re-posting on Instagram is when we basically steal a beautiful image from someone else's account and post it on our own, with loose crediting to the original owner or no crediting at all. Some of us are decent enough to tag the picture to the original user while the rest of us either write #repost without a username or document the image as our own, all ways of which are stealing content from the original users.

We become so envious of the photography that others show that we feel the need to take from them rather than generate original photos ourselves. The more we scroll through Instagram, the more we come across accounts with the same exact images because we all lack originality. We find it easier to pretend to be influencers than to actually take the time to become influencers. For those more devious, instead of directly taking an image, we try to re-enact the images of influencers we find desirable, taking similar selfies or angles of materialistic items in attempts to generate the same number of followers they have. Because of this fraud, many genuine users have been forced to delete their accounts to prevent further identity theft, throwing away their hard work because we cannot find a way to create our own brands.

In my opinion, one of the most manipulative and controversial tactics ever featured on Instagram is the #giveaway. We all know what this is. A so-called "influencer," or even just anyone on Instagram, posts an image with sparkles, pretty colors, and the hashtag #giveaway in large and obnoxious letters. They then proceed to post below their obnoxious image a mega long post that entices other users with a "free gift," that may or may not actually exist, ONLY IF they like the post, comment about how much they like it, and tag at least 3-5 people on the post.

Not only does this allow the manipulative user to generate more likes and comments on their feed, but it also brings in new potential followers as everyone that is tagged now gets notifications from this post, exposing them to more and more posts from the original user. However, how many of these giveaways actually come to fruition?

Do those who promise free vacations or free puppies actually come through with their promises? My guess is, only about 30% of users who boast giveaways actually come through; the rest either make up excuses as to why the giveaways can no longer happen AFTER they have received their well-desired likes and followers, drag out the contest for so long that people eventually forget about the giveaway, or they announce "winners" so people will think the contests were real, when in reality, these "winners" aren't even real people.

Sadly, there's no way for Instagram to catch people who utilize these manipulative tactics unless enough people report them, and even then, Instagram MAYBE looks into it. This deadly competition among users has made the platform become unenjoyable as the ones who end up surviving are the ones who either don't care about trolls and thieves or those who become trolls and thieves.

Desperate to Belong

The George Floyd incident of 2020 has spiraled protests all around America and the world, with chants of "Black Lives Matter" and demands of defunding the police force. For weeks since the incident, protests have risen in every major city with "Black Lives Matter" #BLM signs and graffiti, looting stores, blocking traffic, and creating chaos amongst an already chaotic world. At first glance, it seems as if these crowds of protesters actually care about the matter of respecting black lives. However, how many of them will actually take the time to support this matter when there isn't a protest going on? How many of them refrain from racist jokes when they believe no one's around to listen to their vulgar but honest opinions?

These so-called "activists" and "protesters" only seem to care when they know they have an audience. Scrolling through Instagram during these protests results in a 250% increase in "Black Lives Matter" posts and profile updates, claiming to be concerned and demanding justice for this cause. But, let's face it, unless you're dealing with this injustice directly, or even indirectly, you don't actually give a shit about black lives, just like you don't give a shit about animal rights or environmental health unless there's a protest going on or if the topic is "trendy" and "popular."

We see people with "Black Lives Matter" signs parading around town, but at the same time, they still see blacks as their stereotypes, calling them the N-word and fearing them. We see people with "Stop Animal Abuse" signs, but at the same time, they're killing mice and eating brutally-massacred cows. We see people with "Protect the Environment" signs, but at the same time, we see them littering and polluting the environment with overuse of hairspray products.

We only care about societal issues when we know we can take advantage of them. We want others to see us as "supportive" and "advocates" because we know those titles can boost our social status as people who care. Most "protesters" are only engaged so they can fit in, to have something they can post and brag about. Take away the popularity of the matter, and we see all those Instagram "support" come crashing down.

#obsessed
Instagram Exposes Humanity

Most people on Instagram don't care about human rights; if we did, we wouldn't be bad-mouthing everyone and everything 364 days of the year and speaking up coincidentally only when everyone else seems to care. We try too hard to fit in, and it becomes obvious that we're only frauds.

Instagram protesters jump back and forth between issues they care about because they want others to believe they're important and special, when behind the scenes, they're not even sure what they're supporting half the time. They believe that if they don't support the common cause, then their Instagram and social lives will be ruined because people would hate them for not "being supportive." When it comes time for one person to speak up about a serious cause, such as poverty, that isn't being celebrated and worshipped as royalty, how many Instagrammers will actually speak up?

Controlled by Standards & Rules

"Only post during certain hours of the day to generate the most likes."

"Make sure you have the most popular hashtags so others can find you."

"Use a filter that really shines, and keep these filters consistent so your feed stands out more."

#obsessed
Instagram Exposes Humanity

"Respond to every DM and every comment that graces your account."

"Drown your posts in hashtags because those matter much more than your stupid captions."

"Photoshop out all the blemishes in your photos to match those of other users."

"Spend every waking moment liking posts on Instagram because that's the only way to get your profile noticed."

"Take images of everything you do because people want a story, not a few random posts."

"Dedicate your entire life to Instagram or delete your account."

The majority of users spend their every waking moments dedicated to Instagram, waking up at odd hours in the morning, going to sleep at odd hours at night, and even skipping out on personal responsibilities, such as work and school, so they can post on Instagram at "optimal" hours of the day, since research upon research has been done to show that certain hours of days are the best times to generate the most likes per post.

We become so obsessed with these rules of posting at certain hours, liking 100 posts per hour, responding to every comment even when we're busy or don't want to respond, pretending to be always happy and fake even when we're miserable, and spending thousands of dollars on filters that don't represent our true images of life just so we can keep up with the crowds.

#obsessed
Instagram Exposes Humanity

We become so obsessed with all of these standards that we neglect everything else for this one social app, literally letting machines take over our lives. When Instagram first came out, it was casual and fun, with friends posting images of their special moments whenever they wanted, and they were actually able to put their phones down for days before picking them back up to see how many likes their posts received, unbothered if the number remained low.

Nowadays, we become lunatics when we step away from our phones for even an hour, seeing our batteries dying as the end of the world, and literally locking our phones away or throwing them into the ocean just to prevent ourselves from checking Instagram every minute of every hour. We have transformed from letting Instagram portray the ways we want to live our lives into living our lives solely for Instagram.

Exposing Instagram "Influencers"

"Every Instagram influencer believes his or her life is worth portraying in a documentary or worth writing about in a book. In reality, they're just people with narcissism and a lot to say."

Who are these famous bloggers and influencers we so highly look up to? Celebrities? Motivational speakers? Athletes? Or just ordinary people with normal lives and normal problems like the rest of us? These "influencers" we see prancing around with fake paparazzi are our friends and our colleagues who started using Instagram with the same goals that we did: to connect with others and show off our best selves. However, what makes these ordinary people stand out as different from us? What do they have that makes them influencers compared to what we have? We're all just people, some with more masks and façades than others, with digitally-sculpted bodies, egotistical confidences, and pockets full of cash, but in the end, we're all the same.

Yet, it's these same factors that exclude people that make some of us more likely to become influencers than others. Becoming an influencer focuses less on how valuable, interesting, or important we are as people; becoming an influencer depends solely on how much we have, how much we can alter, and how much we can convince and manipulate. This computerized and web-based world of social networking has forced us to become superficial. It used to be that only celebrities, motivational speakers, and royalty were influencers. Now, the average Joe across the street or the average Jane next door can become our next role model, with a million followers through little to no effort.

Instagram influencers in the modern world have turned to digital alterations to maintain their influencing dreams, Photoshopping every image and buying every expensive outfit, dinner, or trip possible to keep their dream of becoming popular alive, without a care of whether they put themselves into debt.

Fashion gurus who claim to shop on a budget don't actually stick to a budget as they alter thousands of dollars of clothing to make them seem less expensive but still stand out. Travel influencers who claim to travel solo and on the cheap actually have an entire crew behind the scene, spending more than the average person normally would to rent out spaces they can use to take their undisturbed selfies. Foodies aren't actually down-to-earth home cooks as they hire famous chefs to cook for them so they can make their photos stand out by claiming credit for it afterward.

Not everything we see online is what people claim it to be. The people we look up to are either lying to us or burning through some serious cash to make their phony lives appear flawless. They carve out sections of their bodies, include images in photos that aren't meant to be there (such as trees in the Sahara Desert), and enhance even the smallest of images to seize Internet attention. How many of us have seen side-by-side comparisons of Instagram versus Reality, where Instagram shows a beautiful picture of a picnic by the ocean, but Reality shows a toy picnic set next to a puddle of water?

Instagrammers and other social media addicts deceive us into believing that their mundane lives are so much better than our mundane lives. They overextend their efforts to make simple things become worthy of adoring, proving their shallowness and insecurities. "Influencers" devote their entire lives into making sure that we believe their concocted lives are "natural," as if what they portray is how they live their everyday lives. Really? No one can afford to visit a new country every week for 8 years straight without having some sort of trust fund, and no one can afford a designer wardrobe in every photo when they claim to be "lower class."

Additionally, do influencers really expect us to believe that their picture-perfect face and styled hair portray the image of them "just waking up"? Despite the ridiculousness, we still eat it up, not because we actually believe these influencers are impeccable, but because we are envious of their confidence to put themselves out there while we hide ourselves in shame.

> "Those who try their best to be something they're not are the ones who struggle with self-acceptance the most."

Just a few years ago, Instagram released the option for Instagrammers to open business, or creator, accounts, designed for businesses to showcase their products and work. However, shortly after it came out, Instagrammers discovered how to use this option to monetize from their posts by gaining a shit ton of followers and then getting paid for sponsored posts. While some have been authentically successful with this, others have found themselves scrambling to get noticed, buying thousands of fake followers just to meet the criteria of being an influencer so they can get paid for images they steal from someone else.

These "counterfeit influencers" have deceived people into thinking they're actually worth something when they simply resort to lying about their sponsors. No major company really checks up on the legitimacy of who tags them in their profiles. For most people, it isn't even about the money from being sponsored; it's about the exclusivity, the feeling of being able to "achieve" something no one else can. It's about feeling more important than others and the idea of being famous when they're actually not. Becoming an influencer sounds like a feat that takes time and talent to achieve, but really, it's just a popularity contest. These fake influencers buy their way into fame (like many celebrities do), raising colonies of fake followers that can never fully commit to them, and eventually flushing their money down the drain when everything comes crashing down.

Fake influencers appear to have everything that real influencers have, a web-based clientele, the appearance of fame and likeability, and top-notch pictures that seem too good to be true. But, the main difference between fake frauds and real influencers is their army of bots, machine-generated followers that often have no profile pictures, account names constructed from randomly typing on a keyboard, no postings themselves, no likes or followers themselves, and they comment on posts with phrases such as, "sexy," "cool," "okay," "fun," or "great," short, sparse phrases that don't really add anything or make sense.

For those who can afford higher quality bots, they usually end up with even more nonsensical phrases such as, "I like your video" when the post is a photo, "Very sexy queen" when the post is of a man, or "Hahaha, that is so funny" when the post is about someone's death.

Fake influencers sometimes even recruit their friends and family to create false profiles to enhance their accounts so it seems like they have more followers, or they create fifty different email addresses to create fifty different profiles and comment back and forth on the main one, making the original account seem like it has an army of followers, when in reality, it's still just one person. Fake influencers also use stock photos, claiming them as their own, or they simply pull images from anywhere on the Internet and repost them on their profiles, choosing vague images where the person's back is facing the camera so they can play these stolen images off as self-portraits.

Fake influencers know they're fake, for the most part at least. Some have pretended to be influencers for so long that they have forgotten the difference between their real lives and their pretend lives. However, they still hold their heads up as if they are legit, and they present themselves as genuine despite not having an actual crowd, reputation, or sponsorship to back them up. They pretend to have sponsorship offers and post images and live videos on their feeds as if they have a following who will listen to them.

They use Instagram stories to narrate their entire lives, pretending like they are talking to a crowd because Instagram stories do not reveal how many people actually watched the highlights to outside viewers, allowing these fake influencers to cover up that zero people are paying attention to what they have to say. They spend their waking moments gathering tips and ideas from other influencers, real or fake, and pretend to act like them even though none of it matters. Some fake influencers can become so good at faking their social lives that it can become difficult for people to spot who's real and who's fake. For all we know, none of these influencers are really who they say they are.

Falling victim to the world of fake Instagram influencers can prove dangerous to any type of social media brand or presence we are trying to create. It distorts our image as a fraud, a fake, or a counterfeit rather than someone worth paying attention to, and fake influencers who become exposed will forever remain known as imposters on all social media platforms and in life, an unforgiving nature and a huge risk for potential influencers. Pretending to be an influencer with millions of followers will only continue to drain our pockets with no real gain in return and, eventually, we're forced to either give up our social media life or exposed ourselves as frauds as we realize we can no longer keep up with the demands of trying to cover the fact that we have purchased our fame.

An average brand or person trying to generate fame from an online presence without patience and hard work can blow over $200,000 a year on impressions and false hopes from "100% successful advertisements."

It takes years for a typical person to become a true influencer. Though, not everyone possesses this type of patience and continue to pile on thousands of "followers" within months. Their following counts are low and seem astronomical to the lack of content they have on their pages. There has been evidence of increasingly large numbers of Instagram followers overnight, with users swearing that it's their content that have brought in these followers, not their paychecks. Unless we're a celebrity or a phenomenal photographer of an extremely rare specimen (which I doubt we are), it is physically impossible to gain 10,000 followers in under two days. These spikes are usually from accounts with strange names and no followers or posts, dead giveaways that these are purchased bots. However, even for people who haven't bought followers, the occasional bot slips in every now and then because of the nature of showcasing ourselves on the Internet. Still, when 95% of our followers follow the same trend of a terrible name with no pictures, the excuse of "it just slipped in" is no longer valid.

Fake Instagram influencers are too often lured in by the use of hashtags. It is not common knowledge, but the more hashtags a post has, the more these users are targeted by an infestation of bots on their profiles. The standard number of hashtags used per post is usually two to three, five max. However, when we come across a post with over fifty hashtags, they are trying to lure in bots as bots frequently scan for posts with hashtags. Most people also believe that the more hashtags they drown their posts in, the more likely they are to get people to notice them. Unfortunately, hashtags only serve to make users look desperate.

"Love this!"

"Epic!"

"Delightful!"

"Awesome!"

Instagram Influencers are FAKE

Purchasing Instagram followers and likes, or even Facebook and YouTube followers and likes, is a trend that has skyrocketed over the past few years, something so common that influencers and celebrities all over the world use to give their profiles a kick start as users are more likely to visit a profile that has 5,000 followers than one that only has 5. Despite being a tactic that can prove helpful at first, once people begin to buy followers, they become hooked, turning that 5,000 into 50,000, and eventually into 500,000 with a status claim as an "influencer." To make it more tempting, the cost of buying followers has gotten cheaper and cheaper over the years; the cost for 5,000 followers has become the price of a cup of coffee.

But, what's the point? What's the point of having half a million followers, or even 10 million followers, if none of them are real? The feeling of achieving something without any work always triumphs actual achievements because human beings are LAZY! We would much rather pay to have other people do our petty work for us while we take all the credit because the Internet has made it difficult to stay motivated to work toward achievements.

Even when people realize that they are only paying for bots that stick around for a week and then disappear in mass quantities, they still do it because it's so tempting. So many "influencers" have been caught buying a few hundred bots during their times on Instagram, paying for the impression of being successful until they can actually become successful, so much so to the point where we can no longer distinguish which of our followers are real and which are fake.

We buy so many followers that when these bots begin to drop off, we find ourselves compensating with more and more until we are elbow deep in debt. Bots will never interact with our profiles unless we buy comments and likes also, and even then, those are all still fake.

"Instagram started off as a social network to connect with others. The bots that have taken over have made us lonelier than ever before."

#obsessed
Instagram Exposes Humanity

Many Instagram influencers have devoid themselves of true interactions. They don't care who's actually watching them or not as long as the few who are know that they are "the best" due to their large following. Buying likes and followers can never help an image or a brand grow. Of those 100,000 followers we have posted on our Instagram accounts, maybe only 10 of them are real, 10 real followers who quickly unfollow us when they see that out of 100,000 followers, we only have 5 likes. Bots provide no value, but then again, Instagram is all a number's game.

Even if these influencers aren't purchasing bots day and night, they still portray an image online that does not accurately represent human life. They give people false hope of being able to go anywhere and do anything they want with minimal effort and struggle, all while wearing designer dresses, when we all know that can never happen. Influencers pretend to support matters they don't actually care about just because they want to uphold a positive image, and they forget how to be real. They waltz around as if life is perfect and that everyone envies them, when they are probably miserable inside and struggling to keep up with the demand from their audiences.

"Are they really happy? Or are their smiles all forged?"

The images and faces we see on the Internet do not always mirror the images and faces that are hiding behind the cameras. No one wants to showcase a boring life at a 9 to 5 job, eating a simple sandwich because we are in a rush, or running into areas of foreign countries where we feel unsafe because those aren't the "glamorous lives" we want others to associate us with. We all want to put our best feet forward by showcasing the lives that we want, with others believing that we have amazing lives rather than the lives we actually live.

Because of this, these so called "influencers" expend all their money and energy on lives that they may not even believe in anymore but still struggle to keep up with just to fit in with the rest of the world. These influencers started off their careers because they truly loved what they were doing. Inevitably, the attention and fame that eventually caught up with them made them feel more powerful and under the pressure to keep up or crumble. This is especially true for those who rely solely on their Internet fame and appearances as their source of income.

"Imagine feeling under the weather but still pressured to have to carefully construct that perfect face and go climb that mountain we dread climbing."

"Imagine obtaining huge amounts of debt but still feeling the need to have to fly to that next 'promised dream country' or risk losing thousands of followers."

"Imagine hitting rock-bottom and becoming so desperate to keep up with the raging crowd that we're almost forced to Photoshop our entire lives or go places/do things that the crowd wants us to do rather than the things we love doing."

Hobbies have quickly turned from showcases of true interests to a constructed book of made-up fantasies that fool no one but the self. Despite becoming drained from how much trickery we impose on ourselves and others, we push on because we see our competitors continuing to post lavish images and beautiful selfies, gloating humbly about how special they are, that we feel the heaviness to also do the same.

Regardless of how perfect an image appears to be, it doesn't always reflect the happenings behind the scenes. Grinning selfies and loving couples don't always reflect reality. How many times have we seen dozens and dozens of images of people with blown-up shots of their engagement rings, with their fiancés in the far background and #special, #happilyeverafter, #engagedbitches, #bridetobe, #blessed, and #bflovesme? These images are designed to make us become envious of them because seeing those images makes our loneliness kick in, causing us to crave engagements and love lives of our own. We fool ourselves into wanting the lives that the newly-engaged have, taking wedding photos in the Maldives and having celebrities officiate their weddings, but do we actually want them?

What do you think is going on behind the scenes of big diamond rings and plastic surgeries? How much do you think people pressure their significant others into proposing to them and buying them the heaviest carat they can find JUST so they have something worthy of posting, or should I say, bragging about, on the 'gram. Let's face it, having a small wedding in a small church with a small group of people and a small ring is nowhere near as Instagram-worthy as lavish weddings that allow people to talk about them for months, filling their Instagram feeds with beautiful images of weddings cakes, flower bouquets, expensive venues, and pictures of wedding dress after wedding dress after wedding dress.

Over 70% of Instagram weddings don't last because people end up focusing more on their posts than their relationships, dragging around and controlling their partners so they can generate more followers by showing off things they foolishly believe others wished they themselves had. We only showcase our love lives to the public because we feel insecure about them. We think that by openly talking about them, we solidify that they actually exist, and we think that by taking selfies with our partners who stand next to us looking miserable, others can see how "in love" we actually are.

Those who share their "love" to the world aren't actually in love behind the cameras. Those who are truly in love would much rather share their love with each other in private than feel the need to drag the rest of the universe into it. Couples who appear happy in front of the camera are probably fighting and arguing nonstop once the cameras turn off. How many love lives will still exist when we take away social media? How many people will be exposed for "loving" just so they have something to post online?

The more time we spend on Instagram and comparing our lives to it, the more toxic it proves to ourselves. Instagram doesn't help us feel closer to our friends and loved ones like we all thought it would when we first joined back when it was released. Instead, Instagram makes us feel like shit about ourselves because we're always bombarded with the pressure to do more even when we're already doing our best, with constant harassments telling us that our best will never be good enough. We become so consumed by it, allowing it to become the first thing we look at when we wake up in the mornings and the last thing we look at before we fall asleep at nights. We become addicted with trying to get ahead of others that we begin to resent the lives we have outside of the Internet.

The "influencers" who we admire so much are not always as "perfect" and as "happy" as they appear. In most cases, they try too hard to show off how great their lives are compared to others. Those who are truly content with their lives don't feel the need to show them off. They're satisfied with who they are and continue living as is. Yet, many influencers feel the need to show others how happy they are doing the things they love because it's all a façade. We know this because we see travel influencers lugging 70lbs of camera equipment and crew around, taking selfies and videos of themselves talking about how much they're enjoying these foreign countries instead of actually enjoying them.

They don't showcase their lives because they're proud of them; they do it because they want to show others that they're so much better than them and can achieve successes that many others cannot. Instagram influencers who spend their sole focus on showing off their originality and happiness are the ones who are the most distraught, feeling the need to use distraction after distraction to forget how miserable they actually are. Influencers with over a million followers can become so disconnected from themselves, as they spend their entire time trying to connect with others, that they will become lost the day Instagram goes extinct, and like all social media platforms that come and go, it will. The more followers these influencers have online, the less they're likely to have in real life.

Faking happiness and joy are signs of psychological malnourishment and disturbance because we forget who we're pretending for. We forget that we're parading around in skimpy outfits and blowing our money on lavish vacations and makeovers just to impress people we don't even know. We forget that, despite how many people comment about how lovely our posts are, they don't actually care about us. Half of them are only commenting for hopes of receiving comments and likes back, and the other half are only commenting out of sheer boredom.

But we don't see that! We don't see that we're posting selfies of ourselves in lingerie to nobody except for creeps and perverts! On average, decent and normal human beings spend roughly 5 seconds per post they come across unless it's posts from people they are obsessed with. Most of the time, influencers are only faking their happiness for themselves.

"People who spend more time connecting with themselves are more satisfied than people who spend their time connecting with their phones."

"People who cherish the richness of life are happier than those who are desperate for love and attention."

"Minimalism has proven to generate more positivity in life than materialism."

"Competition does not hurt those who are truly proud of themselves and know themselves."

"Instagram can only destroy those who allow it or rely on it to control their lives."

"Can engineered happiness ever triumph true happiness?"

We live in a world where we have been taught the factors of life that's supposed to make us happy rather than allowing us to choose our own happiness. We associate happiness with a price tag and with quantity, vast quantities of followers, vast quantities of materialism, and vast quantities of money.

We have been brainwashed to believe that we cannot be truly happy unless we have everything and unless we have more than others around us do. We falsely believe that fancy parties and yachts dictate how likeable and important we are. We genuinely believe money can buy us happiness because we haven't put down our phones long enough to discover what really makes us happy.

"Influencers are the blemishes of the social media world."

"If an influencer stops eating, we also feel the need to stop eating."

"If an influencer sips champagne in France, we feel tempted to book a one-way ticket."

"If an influencer spends 8 hours a day at the gym, we automatically sign up for a membership we know we will never use."

"If an influencer wears an outfit that receives 60,000 likes, we run out to buy the same outfit."

"We live the lives of influencers because we're afraid of being left out."

"We live the lives of influencers because we do not love ourselves."

#fittingin

#obsessed
Instagram Exposes Humanity

Instagram influencers are basically makeup artists with a fat brush of concocted lies and games to show the world. They spend so much time building up this online image that they never really take the time to focus on any other parts of their lives. Influencers live by their profiles, blowing all their money and time investing in mindless images that can all disappear one day.

"What happens when Instagram, or any other social media platform, finally comes to an end?"

"What happens when everyone decides to unplug?"

"What happens when social sharing networks become a thing of the past?"

"So, what if these influencers are pulling in $5,000 per sponsored post?"

"Will these so-called 'influencers' still have an income when Instagram perishes?"

"What talents will they have to share then?"

"Will they continue influencing?"

"Will they still be doing the things they claim to enjoy doing on Instagram?"

"Or will they immediately be forgotten as they realize that people don't actually care about influencers, seeing them as fakes and threats rather than as human beings?"

The Algorithm of Success

It's not a secret that certain types of people are more well-liked than others in the Instagram world. If you've ever scrolled down the homepage, you can see that pictures of women in bikinis and shirtless men are almost always at the top of the page with the highest number of likes. That is because sex and the idea of sex sell. The so-called "pretty" people, women especially, are always more likely to grab attention than the average-looking people or those who post pictures of objects rather than selfies.

The images of women who show off their asses and cleavage are bound to grab the attention of almost all men because they're either sleazy or find them attractive, as well as the attention of almost all women because they want to be them and need tips on how to become them.

But, this concept is nothing new. External beauty has, and will always, triumph when it comes to the Internet world because people are shallow. Dating apps focus solely on external appearances when users decide to swipe left or right, and Instagram is no different. Profiles who showcase six-pack abs, giant breasts, and model-like faces are more likely to grab attention than beer-bellies, flat chests, and zit-filled faces.

We don't like admitting it, but we all judge others based on how their faces and bodies look. The pretty girls and the muscular guys will always get the most views and the most likes because people feel like they need to like those who fit the standards of beauty. The more we continue to feel this way, the more we feed into the egos of these so-called "influencers," boosting up their profiles just because they're "hot."

We all think that we need to be attractive in order to be liked. We all try to hide who we really are, taking selfies at absurd angles just to show off our best selves, and only showcasing our faces when we have "good days." And because we all think this way, it becomes reality. Even people who aren't traditionally recognized as beautiful, such as overweight people, have blown up in the social media world.

However, the reason is not what we think. We all "love" images of plus-sized models and "big women" not because we think they're courageous and brave. We love them because they, too, are showcasing their fake selves, coating themselves in makeup and slim-fitting clothes, pretending to be people they are not, because even they believe that their authentic selves will not be liked. True, there are users who relish in the accounts of actual #nofilter images, but there is also always a crowd who will judge others despite what and who they post. We are judgmental by nature.

Admit it. The reason we refrain from being so openly judgmental on the Internet and refuse to be completely honest is because we don't want to stand out as being opinionated and risk societal hatred. Imagine opening up a post and seeing hundreds of positive comments about some random stranger sitting at the beach. We don't want to be the first ones to say something negative about the photo, even if we think it, because then we'll be seen as "haters" and warrant dislikes and unfollows. However, if we see hundreds of positive comments but also a small handful of negative ones, we have no problem expressing how we truly feel if we think the photo is hideous because then we'll know we're not alone and, therefore, will not be ostracized.

Mainstream media has promoted unrealistic beauty for years, more so since the rise of Photoshop, portraying stick-thin fashion models and chiseled celebrities in place of feasible bodies. This unrealistic portrayal of women and men has caused deadly consequences since, as models and gymnasts began starving themselves for their careers, and young boys and girls developed eating disorders trying to look like their icons. The world of social media has destroyed healthy self-esteem and body image, with Instagram playing right into the game. Altered body images now become common for gaining followers with curated Instagram feeds channeled toward making ourselves more likeable, yet, also more depressed.

Instagram forces us to parade around half-naked and post pictures of our external bodies on our profiles because it manipulates us into believing that those images get results. Because of how desperate we are, we go for it and expose our naked bodies online even when we don't want to. We willingly post nudes because we have been brainwashed to believe that people will like us more if we do so. This has gotten so bad that some people have taken advantage of this and utilize Instagram as their own personal porn stash.

The world of catfishing has also blown up as people started becoming less and less confident in themselves as being able to generate likes and followers as they are. They believe that if they don't pretend to be someone more approachable or more beautiful, then they'll never have the chance to become influencers, or even someone with more than 20 followers. Many influencers aren't fully themselves; some people pretend to be someone else completely. Others only post images of their backsides so people can never tell what they actually look like, and the rest of these Instagram influencers Photoshop so much on every picture that not even they can recognize what they really look like anymore. But how can they stay on top otherwise?

But, remember, likes toward posts that achieve desired attention are usually only directed toward one part of the image, the face, the ass, the boobs, the abs, the money, etc. These "devoted followers" who we all believe loyally follow and worship us are only attracted to parts of us, the shallow parts, rather than the entire picture. When someone likes our picture, it doesn't necessarily mean they like us; they just like the parts of us that they see. Over 80% of Instagram users who like posts don't even take the time to read what the posts say. They react with their eyes, and if they see something they like, they click "like," even if the posts mention murder or infidelity.

Innovation to Self-Reinvention

As Instagram grows, so do the people who claim to love the same things influencers do. Five years ago, there was only a small handful of influencers in each category, whether it's travel, fashion, fitness, or food. However, as the platform became more and more popular, we begin to see all these micro-influencers rise from nowhere, micro-influencers with small colonies of followers, racing for the higher positions.

These micro-influencers live life solely for Instagram and try too hard to showcase every experience and every part of their lives. They strive to stand out by pulling followers from every direction despite what it takes, including buying followers and #follow4follow. They also spend hours researching and stalking verified influencers to see how they can reach up to their grandeur and status, regardless of whether these popular influencers are real people. They are usually the most insecure and often the ones more likely to fake their way through posts and copy verified influencers to stand out. This also makes them more likely to Photoshop their images and alter their videos.

Despite how hard we try, standing out amongst the influencer crowds just isn't enough. It has gotten to the point where we need to stand out from ALL THE CROWDS, including engaging in death-inducing and epic activities, where lives become at stake for who wins the biggest influencer crown. However, the problem lies in that the more these micro-influencers draw in the crowds that support them, the more pressured they feel to have to keep up with the demand, forcing them to change their original motives into something that pleases more than just one group of people. This causes influencers to go from showcasing what they love to what they feel they need to post in order to keep their positions as "the best."

"As an influencer, when I post something on Instagram, and it doesn't get 500 likes within the first hour, I delete it, pour my heart into more research on what sells, re-examine my angle, blame myself for not being as good as other influencers, and keep re-posting until my followers give me what I want. If my posts don't make me feel special and important, I beat myself up over

them, become self-destructive, and either quit Instagram
forever or open another (better) account."

Nevertheless, let's not solely point fingers at influencers
who try too hard. What about their "faithful" supporters,
the users, the trolls? The average person plays a much
bigger role in the Instagram world than the influencers
themselves because average people influence how
influencers will create their next posts. Without average
people to follow them, influencers would not exist.

People's desires change all the time. We may want travel
pictures one minute from one influencer and then want
that same influencer to become a bikini model, and in
order to keep their followers, influencers give the crowds
what they want, at their own demise. These new users are
the ones who impact social media the most, manipulating
influencers into posting what they want to see with false
promises of following them. One strong voice can quickly
turn an influencer's profile from 2 million followers to
200.

Influencer Attraction and Reputation

"We see these beautiful people in these beautiful places, and we automatically assume that their lives are as glamorous as their photoshoots."

"We see lavish cars and designer clothing and believe they come from wealth."

#obsessed
Instagram Exposes Humanity

"We see a new photo of a new country every other day and believe they are living the dream life of traveling the world."

"We see their smiles every day and believe they have it all together."

"Glamorous images are often doctored or fake."

"Lavish cars and designer clothing can often be followed closely by debt."

"New country photos can mean luxury backdrops and green screens."

"Smiles can often have tears behind the screens."

I'm sure we can all agree that looking our best is the way to go when it comes to posting images. We even post our #freshoutofbed selfies with a face full of makeup and a perfect hairdo. We know that the minute we post a truly authentic no filter and no makeup image, we will receive 5x more dislikes than likes. We lie to ourselves that we need to be incredible and outstanding in order to feel good about ourselves even if our followers disagree.

Some people take this mindset way too far, mistaking "ridiculous and offensive" as "glamorous and beautiful." Instagram influencers often try too hard to grab the attention of the crowd that they forget how to be genuine. They allow their psychological rationality to become affected because the more they feel insecure about losing their followers, the more they become desperate to change their appearances. They develop an intense obsession with altering photos and acting exploitative and dishonest for the sake of advancing and being the best.

No amount of exercise or even plastic surgery will give us the images we proclaim are #100%real, and people know many of these are fake. The Internet may be gullible and weak, but it isn't stupid. People on the Internet all know (for the most part) that these falsified images are actually a hoax; they are just too scared to be the first ones to call out these powerful influencers on them and risk being branded as #unpopular and #troll.

On the other hand, let's take a moment to consider the influencers who actually have authentic photos. How do they achieve such amazing photos all the time without massive photo editing? I recently got the chance to catch up with a travel influencer I once knew while I was also part of the Instagram crowd. In order to capture these beautiful photos of famous tourist sites without all crowds, she has to wake up before the crack of dawn, multiple mornings in a row, due to uncertainties in weather conditions and other extraneous circumstances, and carry her entire camera set with her (all 50lbs of it) to her destinations, even if it means having to hike up mountains with heavy equipment and heels, all without getting herself dirty.

After spending over an hour setting up her equipment, she takes over 100 images of herself and then spend more hours sorting through them for the best ones, adding vivid filters over her images, and writing the perfect captions. If those weren't enough, most of her "amazing images" consist of layering, where she would take an image of her desired backdrop and an image of herself, separately, and stich the two together, making it seem as if her personal self is front of the beautiful backdrops. As an Instagram influencer, over 12 hours of her day, every day, is devoted to Instagram posts. With only 300,000 followers and the unknown potential of Instagram crashing any day, is all this hard work really worth it, or is it all for superficial attention?

While a lot of people on Instagram are fake, there are many who prove that being an influencer isn't as simple and easy as their images make it seem. A lot of effort goes into creating the perfect image, and there's bound to be stress along the way when we end up losing more than we gain, especially for fresh influencers who are trying to make a name for themselves. In the end, only the strong prevail, the ones who truly care about their worth as opposed to just their numbers, while those who are only in it to win it either become discouraged or bored.

A Perpetual Competition

When we look at social media accounts, such as on Facebook and Instagram, what's the purpose of even having one? The intention for such sites should be to connect with those we haven't seen in a long time or to connect with new friends. However, how often does that happen? Sure, there are people, especially those in their middle ages, who actually care about using the outlet for said reasons, but human beings are driven by competition. We fail to see our lives as worth living unless we have something to prove and show others.

We are social creatures who, unless we are able to compete and show off our winnings and greatness over those of others, we struggle to find worth and meaning in life. For example, if no one is watching, if no one is around to see or hear us do the great things we claim to be doing, would we still do them? Would we still enjoy doing them? Are these hobbies still part of our beings and worth our time if we had no one to share them with?

"Social media is a place for us to brag about the things we're not actually doing so people will think we're not just sitting around all the time."

"Social media is a place for us to one up our friends and colleagues, showing them that we really did 'accomplish' all that we said we would ten years ago."

"Social media is a place for us to run one 5k race and show off our medal and athletic skills, excluding the time that it actually took for us to run it."

"Social media is a place for us to show off our new romantic partners, hashtagging how happy we are, when in reality, we're fighting 70% of the time, only stopping long enough to take a staged photo."

"Social media is a place for us to have accomplishments and do everything we can to rub them in the faces of others, whether it's winning an award or getting a job promotion."

"There's only so many angles of a piece of paper that we can take before it's time to move on."

We think that when we post on the Internet about how awesome we are, that people will immediately become super jealous and want to be us. And it's true. We see how great others are doing and feel left behind. We want to experience accomplishments also in order to beat our friends because no one likes being the "loser" of the party. We start doubting what we're doing with our lives, why we're not that famous musician that our friend is, why we're still stuck in an entry-level position when our co-worker is moving up, and why we're still Internet dating and bumming around when our sibling is happily married with two kids. And even if we didn't think we're losers before, we definitely start thinking we are after comparing ourselves to others and indirectly hearing that we have done nothing while others have done everything.

Not that I'm innocent of any of this, but I once knew someone who would just start recording everything she did in her day to day. I mean, everything, from the moment she woke up with elegant brunches to the moment she shopped at Saks Fifth Avenue in her gold Porsche with $5,000 daily clothing and accessory purchases to the moment she went out to expensive steakhouses with her boyfriend while flaunting her new engagement ring to the moment she fell asleep under the stars while lying on a beach in Hawaii. Great life, right?

It shouldn't be, because none of it was real. In reality, her breakfast consisted of a stale bagel in the car with spilled coffee, an office job where she slaved in a cubicle next to a man who sang off-key, drove an old 2004 Toyota Corolla, returned all the clothes that she bought, paid someone to be her new hot steady long-term fiancé, and basked on a beach along the Jersey shore, cropping out the backdrop. She played it off as truth for about three months, ran out of vacation days and stopped posting on the Internet completely. Her reasoning? She was "currently tired" from dealing with her busy social life and decided to take a break from social media.

This just goes to show, not everything we see online is a true representation of how someone is. All of or none of what we see can be real. We can be anyone or anything we want to be, or at least portray ourselves that way. Want to be a musician? Hit up Guitar Center and take a sick photo of yourself "strumming." Want to be a mountaineer? Take a selfie at the base of a mountain and chronicle about how you climbed and summited successfully. Want to be a competitive runner? Borrow a bib and have someone take a picture of you near the finish line.

No one needs to know or will know that we lie on our pictures unless they really look into them, which no one actually does. We go through more effort to look like we have accomplished something than it would've taken to actually do it. And, nowadays, people have gotten so skilled at Photoshop that it has become effortless to be anywhere in the world without having to spend a single dime. So many of the images on the highly-trafficked pages we see on Instagram are Photoshopped. How do I know? I don't! That's the problem!

However, this #fakeittillyoumakeit and #friendlycompetition are also gateways for the increasing rate of suicide caused by virtual stress and cyberbullying. According to the World Health Organization (WHO),

#obsessed
Instagram Exposes Humanity

1.54 million people die from suicide every year, with a good fraction of that correlated to online-related drama. These suicide rates are known to have been influenced by not only personal factors, but social and environmental factors as well. As people become more pressured to fit in with the social media crowd, their emotional and mental health issues begin to take a toll for the worst.

Cyberbullying is no joke. This increasing problem has been linked to more suicide-related deaths than any other online matter, affecting mostly vulnerable, younger generations all trying to reach for that common goal of fame and fortune without having to do any of the work but post selfies. Sickeningly, it has become a trend for younger generations to harm themselves or commit suicide LIVE on their social media platforms, with their audiences cheering and booing rather than calling the cops, a shocking awakening for current and future generations.

The media loves to popularize and portray dangerous behaviors and toxic images that distort the minds of young individuals as they lose sight of what they should be following. Instagram provides higher risks for young adults as they promote pro-suicidal sites, message boards for planned homicides, and chat rooms and forums that allow groups of sick-minded individuals to come together and plot against others because the exclusivity makes them believe they can.

And if that isn't bad enough, users on Instagram all around the world are more likely to support these groups and ideas rather than prevent them because online presence allows people to say and support matters they wouldn't normally. We play these major roles in the deaths of innocent people, but at the same time, we pretend to feel sad and remorseful when these people actually do die, mourning with the rest of the Internet so we can feel a sense of belonging.

"Your Instagram presence is causing the death of another human being."

Unfortunately, online stupidity can be just as deadly as online bullying and cults. We find joy in seeing risky images on Instagram, such as taking selfies in front of a moving train and selfies while jumping off buildings with no experience, and without even thinking whether these images are real, we attempt to recreate them, landing ourselves in hospitals and death by attempting these same feats no sane human being would do. #YOLO

We also fall for gimmicks of challenges that would otherwise make no sense to us, including the Fire Challenge, the Ghost Pepper Challenge, and the Tide Pod Challenge. For those of you who are lucky enough to be unaware of these challenges, forgive me for exposing you to them now. The Fire Challenge is when we cover our bodies in flammable liquids and then set the liquids on fire, causing us to turn into a walking fireball, or a pile of ash, whichever one sounds more appealing. The Ghost Pepper Challenge is when we devour an entire ghost pepper, known as the hottest pepper in the world, without allowing ourselves to drink any milk to prevent our tongues from burning off. Finally, the Tide Pod Challenge, probably one of the more recent and memorable ones, is when we purchase toxic detergent Tide pods from the grocery store and eat them because the Internet tells us they are delicious while we end up in hospitals an hour later to have our stomachs pumped.

This is also not just exclusive to Instagram; people do these crazy and insane challenges all over the world on all forms of social media, not realizing how stupid they are even after they end up in critical care. Hospitalizations have skyrocketed since the last decade because more and more teenagers are landing themselves in emergency rooms for trying out acts they see on the Internet.

"In 2008, a Japanese forum shared that people can kill themselves using gaseous hydrogen sulfide. Because people have a habit of idolizing suicidal and homicidal behaviors, especially when they are portrayed online, shortly after, over 200 people attempted to kill themselves using gaseous hydrogen sulfide, with a 95% success rate." #suicide

Craving a Stranger's Attention

"FOMO = fear of missing out"

"Phubbing = ignoring the person you're talking to so you can look at your phone"

Is social media to blame for our downfall in mental health and drastic increases in depression and anxiety? In 2018, a research group at the University of Pennsylvania performed an experiment on a group of undergraduates, where they limited their use of social media, Facebook, Snapchat, and Instagram included, to only 10-minutes a day while also measuring their resulting levels of depression. What they found was that spending less time on Instagram and other social media platforms a day can be part of the answer in how we can reduce our depression statistics.

"Our discoveries unequivocally recommend that restricting Internet-based life use to around 30 minutes a day may prompt critical improvement in prosperity."

Every day, we are distracted by the biosphere of social media. We allow notifications of someone liking our post or a new photo of someone we are following distract ourselves from reality. We check our phones the first thing in the morning and the last thing at night. We check our phones even as we are in critical conditions such as in car accidents and emergency rooms. We have let these pop-up notifications run our lives, and 95% of the time, these are notifications we don't even care about, yet, we drop everything we're doing to check them.

"Instagram can literally kill us."

We continue to check our feeds even when we're unsure of what we're checking; most of the time, we just feel the need to check for the sake of checking. We instinctively reach for our phones all hours of the day, when we're on a date, when we're in a meeting, when we're at the gym, and even at our own weddings. It's as if we feel possessed to reach for our phones every several minutes or, otherwise, we'd combust and explode. Millions of Instagram users actually become surprised when they find out how many hours a day they actually devote to this social media platform.

#obsessed
Instagram Exposes Humanity

Picking up our phones every minute will not help us win a million dollars nor will it help us succeed in life. The only results that endless hours of perusing on Instagram can achieve are anxiety and misery as we see low counts of likes and comments from trolls.

But, is social media to blame for our obsessions with Instagram and our risk-taking behaviors, or do we just suck as willpower and allow others to convince us into doing things we don't normally do, way too easily? Can we ever stop being under the influence of social media? Can we ever learn to just put our phones down for an entire day without sweating tears? Can we ever just unplug and live life without feeling the need to share every part of ourselves with others as if others even care?

Instagram Landmarks

Instagram photos with perfect backdrops have become the new version of selfies with celebrities. Nowadays, people don't even take the time to look at our profiles unless we are in a room surrounded by marshmallows, absorbed by twinkling lights, or have the entire city skyline below us. And even then, we may still not get noticed. We always see these images of influencers with the same backdrops, such as hanging for their dear lives on Brazil's Pedra de Gavea, a cliff where people can hang off and pretend they are dangling a thousand feet in the air, when in reality, they are two inches from another rock below them.

But, because of this enticing photo opportunity, there are often long lines piled up with people hoping to snag this picture for the 'gram. But this is not even the worst of it. In more recent years, dangerous mountains, like Mount Everest, have become top of the list for photo ops, a dangerous endeavor. With hundreds of people dying every year, scaling Mount Everest is difficult enough in itself as oxygen supplies are slim the closer to the peak. If you've ever seen images of people climbing Mount Everest, you will notice that there's usually only one route up, forcing crowds to wait in line, diminishing their supplies. Now, imagine that but with dozens upon dozens of hopeful Instagrammers per day snapping selfies and posing for the perfect Instagram image as they near the summit. Not only do they put themselves at risk by losing oxygen, but other climbers below them are putting their lives at risk waiting for these ignorant climbers to finish taking pictures of something they may or may not even get to post.

But, fear not! Society has developed (and learned to monopolize) on how to offer opportunities for fantastic photo ops without the risks of death. Over the past several years, museums have popped up all over the world that feature rooms where people can go into one by one, where they are surrounded by beautiful and artificial scenery designed JUST for the sake of wowing the Instagram world and gaining those beloved followers.

Some of these museums include the Museum of Ice Cream in San Francisco, where rooms are coated in shades of pink and people can pretend to ride animal cookie carousels, the Color Factory located in both San Francisco and New York, which features an explosion of a rainbow, as if people really did eat a bag of Skittles, and includes a swimming pool of yellow balls, and Candytopia, the pop-up museum located in (you guessed it!) San Francisco and New York where Instagrammers can become surrounded by all the sweets they can imagine as if it's Willy Wonka's Chocolate Factory, and where even people who are diabetic post images with #kidinacandyfactory or #sweettooth. The creators of these museums know what people want, engineering lights, fountains, indoor galaxies, and even rooms full of fake llamas to give people the opportunity to brag on their Instagram...and everybody falls for them.

Instagram's quick and effortless ability to easily showcase fake lives have put fear into the CEOs of other social media platforms such as Twitter. People fall in love with their eyes, and if they see a page of pretty colors and beautiful scenery, why wouldn't they choose that over a page of unfiltered shots featuring drug epidemics? Sometimes, people find it difficult to come up with the best captions to say, finding a great photo of themselves they want to post but struggle to find the words to go with it. With Instagram, this struggle disappears. Instagram accentuates imagery and symbolism so users are able to just take a picture, post it, and get thousands of likes without even having said a single world as we are often limited to a certain number of characters and given only one chance to wow the world in 20 words or less.

Have you ever walked into a famous historical site, such as the Westminster Abbey in London, the Sistine Chapel in Rome, or the Van Gogh Museum in Amsterdam, pulled out your phone, and have been disappointed when you're told that photography isn't allowed? Since the rise of Instagram, famous sites such as the New York's Metropolitan Museum of Art and the Boston Museum of

Fine Arts have changed their rules on "no-photographs," now allowing photography into the buildings for those who have been dying to capture selfies in front of beautiful art.

We have been so persuaded by Instagram, feeling the need to take a picture of and post everything we see, that we become confused when we come across a place that confiscates our cameras as we try to use them. We have been so accustomed to taking lavish selfies that we no longer register that there are going to be other people around us as we take our pictures, and that we're not allowed to tell them to get the fuck out while we take our shots. We become so focused on our own little Instagram worlds that we forget that a real world exists beyond just ourselves. Landmarks and historic sites don't exist for the purpose of allowing us to have a bangin' Instagram.

During my travels through Asia, I visited famous landmarks such as the Angkor Wat in Cambodia, the Grand Palace in Thailand, and the Great Wall of China in, well, China. Rather than admiring these beautiful places, I was faced with more people than not either posing for selfies in front of them or experiencing these places through their phones, seeming more excited about allowing their followers to see how "happy" and lucky they are to be in these places than enjoying these rare moments themselves. Many Instagrammers never enjoy the places they travel to, the food they eat, or the clothes they wear because they do them all for Instagram.

I once knew someone who was always perfectly content wearing t-shirts and sweatpants until she joined Instagram as a fashion guru. Don't ask me why. But, six months into her journey of becoming an influencer, she had blown over

$20,000 on clothes alone that she would only wear for her pictures. She dressed better for her Instagram pictures than she did for her brother's wedding! We dedicate our lives to Instagram, selling our souls and our bodies just to become #instafamous. Pretty soon, like all social media platforms, Instagram will be replaced. What will these influencers have accomplished then? How will they make their living when they can no longer exploit themselves for cash over the Internet?

Selfie Armageddon

Taking that "perfect" photo can be just as easy as smiling or just as dangerous as dangling off a cliff, as long as users have the filters and Photoshop skills to polish it up afterward. It's actually shocking how scary some people's Photoshopping skills can be! We can see two famous adventurist influencers side-by-side, and while one is actually jumping off cliffs and dangling off helicopters, the other is jumping off beds and dangling off monkey bars.

Some influencers can spend their whole Instagram careers on Photoshop, never leaving their homes but still living the lives they claim to have because they can simply lie. We relish in people living lives that are not real, and we kill ourselves trying to be like them. We follow accounts that are heavily filtered more than we follow real accounts. We care more about living vicariously through other people's photos than we do trying to make something of ourselves, defending these influencers when they receive a bad comment like we know them like the back of our own hands.

Selfies have blossomed in the world of social media, boosting the term "egotistical" to a whole different level. We all know what selfies are, though some of us love them more than others. Selfies are when we take that camera or that phone and take pictures of ourselves instead of other things or other people. We position ourselves in our best angles, showing our best duck faces, and take over fifty images of the same face just to hate all of them except for one. You know who you are. Despite only being a few years old, selfies have become a normal part of everyone's lives.

Even though we think that selfies help us promote self-love and self-acceptance, what selfies actually do is further enhance our insecurities and emotional issues, aka, the more selfies we take, the more we do not love ourselves. Those who have true acceptance toward themselves do not need validation from strangers AFTER they have meticulously constructed the best images of themselves to show. It's self-destructive! This over-the-top behavior is simply a coping mechanism for people to feel good about themselves after lacking confidence, and seeking validation from others to fill the emptiness they feel for themselves.

#obsessed
Instagram Exposes Humanity

"According to the American Psychiatric Association, there are three levels of selfie addiction: fringe (taking three selfies a day), intense (taking three consecutive selfies a day), and interminable (taking at least 6 selfies a day)." Hell, most of us consider even 6 a day as too little.

All around the world, people are snapping selfies, with women more likely than men, people in suburban areas more likely than in urban areas, and more likely on the western part of the world than the eastern part, with 61.6% of women obsessed with selfies in New York but only 55.2% in Bangkok, and an incredible 82% in Moscow. However, similar to checking Instagram eight times every hour, people feel compelled to take selfies, when they feel ugly, when they feel threatened, when they see places that look too enticing to not have a photo in, and especially when they feel bored. Look through an average person's phone. I guarantee you you'll see at least ten recent selfie images.

Like all other addictions, selfie addiction is a major problem. Yes, it's a thing. People can become so hooked on taking selfies that it becomes all they know and want to do. Take Danny Bowman, for example, a 19-year-old British high school student who became obsessed with taking selfies, fixating on it more than the rest of his life. He couldn't see past his actions other than wanting to take selfies, taking over 200 selfies every day, destroying his social life, and eventually dropping out of school. Who knew that being obsessed with selfies can destroy your life? In 2014, the story of Danny Bowman was portrayed as a young adolescent who became addicted to selfies, dropped out of school, and attempted to kill himself while going through withdrawal, a heartbreaking story many have failed to learn from.

#obsessed
Instagram Exposes Humanity

Selfie addiction has become so bad that it has given rise to the psychological condition, "selfitis," characterized by a fanatic enthusiasm to crave taking photographs of the self and posting them on social media-based platforms for the world to see as a way of compensating for the lack of confidence. Taking selfies has become a movement. A movement! Contrary to common knowledge, taking a selfie is not just as simple as taking a picture of the self. Taking a selfie now comes with enhancements that are required to present the "perfect photo," a photo that differs completely from the image originally taken.

Nowadays, these selfies need to come with evolving filters and foundations that help alter and transform images on a different level before we allow our selfies to become posted on social media. Taking selfies is a way for us to feel good about ourselves when we can see a photo of us we originally think is ugly and then transform it into something amazing, despite whether this transformed image even looks like us anymore. Our selfies allow us to become the people we want to be but think we can never achieve. We become addicted because our self-esteems are so low that we need to create alter egos just to be able to share ourselves with the world.

"We take selfies because we can't stand the way we look in the mirror."

Risking Lives for the Perfect Post

"One couple's Instagram profile has increased by 3,000 followers in one night because of a photo of them skydiving into a volcano."

"Instagram fashion guru gains an incredible 150,000 likes on one single post in one day for her shopping binge around the world, blowing $20,000 on makeup in Milan, $15,000 on shoes in Paris, and $50,000 on handbags in

Monaco, all while claiming a humble allowance of
$50,000 a month."

Why do we go through so much effort, risking our lives
and our futures, just to gain a few hundred followers who
may or may never interact with us? Is it just for the
number, because we all know that maybe only about 1%
of these loyal clones, if we're lucky, actually interact with
us? Do we do it to boost our self-esteems? Can they really
be boosted if we're suffering in other ways? Or do we do
it out of envy, feeling doubtful about our own lives so we
pretend to be others when we see images of them on lavish
vacations or fancy dinners with their gorgeous partners
and perfect outfits, and we feel like we're missing out on
life by not living like them, giving ourselves mentalities that
there's something wrong with our lives even when we
didn't originally think so? #statusofmind

We have become so obsessed with trying to capture that
perfect moment that beats out everyone else that we turn
our lives into life-or-death moments. How many times
have you seen posts on Instagram where someone is
dangling off a plane, coming face-to-face with a bear,
hanging with one arm off the top of one of the tallest
buildings in the world, or taking selfies in front of moving
trains and erupting volcanos? These senseless and
dangerous acts would normally not be part of people's
lifestyles, unless they are pure adventurists, but the world
of social media have turned normal people with normal
and mundane lives into people who risk everything they
have just for that #perfectpost.

Influencers are the worst when it comes to uploading
images no one really cares about, from their daily breakfast
food they probably don't eat to every exercise they pretend

to do to awkward yoga postures with pigs on their backs to expensive outfits they only wear once. Still want that charm that comes with being an influencer? Say goodbye to your life. The charm of being an Internet star comes with never truly being able to live the life you want without feeling the need to give others what they want to keep them #loyal. Influencers are at constant wars with their own minds, pulling back and forth between what they want to do and what they should do, compelled to put their lives at risk even when they don't want to, going to extreme measures just for temporary fame.

#socialmediabadass

#doitforthegram

#riskitall

"Do it for the 'gram." Really? We steal, we murder, we DIE, just so we can have something worthy of showing on Instagram?

"Is our life simply only worth one epic photo?"

"Will we die for Instagram?"

People desperate for Internet fame fall off high mountains and buildings regularly while trying to pose for the 'gram in attempts to catch an epic selfie and define themselves as #risktakers before plunging to their deaths. While attempting to take a selfie in Taranto, Italy in front of the beautiful waters, a woman plunged to her death instead as she toppled over and fell on top of sharp rocks. In Portugal, two children witnessed their parents fall to their deaths as they attempted to take a selfie on the edge of a cliff. We see these epic photos and automatically assume they are real, and we attempt to re-create them at our own expenses. Take the Magic Bus, for example, located on the Stampede Trail in Fairbanks, Alaska, where Chris McCandless was found dead during his Alaskan adventure. Since the movie about his life came out, many tourists have fluttered over to that same location for that iconic photo in front of the bus, only to find themselves trapped on the wrong side of the vicious Teklanika River that Alexander Supertramp also found himself, dying in attempts to cross the same dangerous river, never getting that chance to post.

Among the nations with the deadliest selfie occurrences, Russia tops the list with the most fatalities per year. In 2016, a 12-year-old student died while trying to take a selfie of herself hanging off her 17th floor balcony, losing her balance, and tumbling down. A few months before that another student died while trying to climb an electrical tower in Moscow, when he was electrocuted during a selfie pose. If those weren't bad enough, Instagrammers are regularly lured into a toxic lake in Siberia, known for its turquoise waters, but also a dumping ground for chemical waste with a high case of bear sightings. Despite these concerns, when that opportunity comes up for epic Instagram-worthy photos, the thought of, "Shit, I'm going to get mauled by a bear" doesn't really cross our minds; instead, we can only focus on, "I need to get a close shot of myself with the bear."

"Selfies can cost us our lives."

#obsessed
Instagram Exposes Humanity

#obsessed

"The world is completely fixated on Instagram."

The meaning of a photograph has changed since the start of the Instagram nation. Remember the good times of disposable cameras, where we would have to wait weeks to have our pictures printed out at the store? Photographs used to represent a way to treasure real moments in our lives that we want to look back on years later and appreciate.

#obsessed
Instagram Exposes Humanity

Nowadays, we use photographs as a base for how well we can enhance them to become something they're not, how well we can turn our photos into something that others cannot, caring more about what we portray to others in the present moment than what we can reflect back on later. We don't care about saving memories anymore; we only care about making others believe we have memories. We delete our memories when our photos are not well-liked or not good enough, and we create memories based on what others want to see, unable to look at ourselves in the mirror at the end of the day because we didn't take what we wanted for ourselves.

On average, Instagram sees over 4.2 billion likes per day. However, the majority of these likes aren't even genuine likes. The majority of these 4.2 billion likes either come from attempted users' tactics to gain more likes themselves by hoping the accounts they like will like them back or from bots that people pay for to auto-like thousands of images a day to fulfill that same #like4like tactic.

"When we see accounts with over 10,000 likes while we have 10, we become distraught, delete our photos that we have once been so proud of, and delete our lives."

"We put forward photos that we know will make others want to be us."

"We put forward photos that make our exes regret losing us and our crushes regret not being with us."

"We put forward photos that make others see how important and valuable we are compared to them, despite the fact that we're fake."

#obsessed
Instagram Exposes Humanity

"We are willing to do whatever it takes to grab even one #like from one person, including bribing, sending nudes, and making obscene promises."

"We pay people to become our #followers because we fear not being able to get any on our own or not being able to get enough on our own."

"We sleep with sleazes who promise us false fame and influencer status, especially that well-desired #instagramverified status."

We pay strangers to pretend to be our partners because our real partners are not #Instagramhot, blowing thousands of dollars to portray a life that isn't ours. The more commonly known version of this is #Instagramboyfriends, men that women pretend to be with romantically who only exist in their worlds to help them take fantastic images of them holding a floating hand, sitting "casually" on large rocks, flashing their boobs beside a pool, and prancing in fields, all without allowing their "boyfriends" any screen time but with #beaulovesme.

Everyone has become so focused on themselves that people only exist to help Instagrammers boost their online presence. I can't even count how many times I have seen girls twirling in front of cameras with men bored behind the scenes, just to later see these same girls with #caughtoffguard. No, you're not fucking caught off guard, in your $5,000 dress and someone spitting water in your hair to mimic rainfall. This #Romaexperience allows "influencers" to have that #instabeau without any real commitment, a lie they hire to help them rise on the social media platform.

#obsessed
Instagram Exposes Humanity

For those of you unfamiliar with the Carolyn Stritch incident, a #instastar and #blogger famous for her controversial shots of Disneyland, she successfully fooled Instagrammers for over 20,000 likes for her post of her walking through what looked like an abandoned Disneyland in California while wearing a polka dot dress.

However, what her loyal followers didn't know was that rather than actually visiting this popular tourist destination, she plucked a photo from the Internet and simply Photoshopped herself into it. Photoshop and the Roma Experience are just two of the manipulative tactics people use to promote the weakening of psychological well-beings as desperate followers see images that have been falsely promoted as real.

"Those of us who accept ourselves and our failures wholeheartedly without trying to be someone else are the ones most successful in life."

"Instagram represents life. We become vulnerable and put ourselves out there even when we know there's a chance of getting hurt. However, when we do get hurt or when we find out people do not like us, we try a different method. We try being someone else, dressing up our bodies and faces to look like someone far different than who we are to begin with, looking like the people who gets the most attention and worship, all while feeling miserable and depressed on the inside. At the end of the day, we drink ourselves to sleep because we cannot stand who we have become. We pass out, wake up, and repeat this again."

We always see the same pattern, pretty girls and muscular boys, posting the same photos as everybody else but still remaining on top because of their external attractiveness. These unrealistic images of blemish-free faces, 0% body fat, and backgrounds without even a crack on the concrete have become the quintessential norm for posting. Nevertheless, at the end of the day, fakes will always continue being fakes and doing what they want with their time and lives; as long as we don't give into these concocted images, we can save ourselves from social media depression, and these so-called "influencers" will eventually fall.

Stop focusing so much of your time on Instagram. Unless you're a sponsored influencer, these hashtags you throw out on every post aren't going to help you accomplish anything. A shit ton of followers who don't even talk to you and an increasing number of hearts aren't going to save your life one day.

We spend all our time on social media and Instagram. Great! Let's continue that when we're homeless. All social media influencers, as popular as they seem now, will eventually be forgotten, with nothing left to prove their existences with because they have done nothing else with their lives other than post pictures. Having one follower versus one million followers is not going to change a thing if there's no reward at the end of the line. Instagram is a constant competition with no winner and many losers.

Deception for Acceptance

Photoshopping images used to be looked down upon. We saw magazine covers with parts of Beyonce's and Lady Gaga's bodies shaved off and riots broke out because of this injustice for altering images to fit the conventional standards of beauty. Just a few years down the line, Photoshopping has become the norm, an almost-expected if we want to stand out and keep up with the world. We are quick and eager to take lessons on the basics of

Photoshop, but only just enough to make sure our followers do not disappear.

Unfortunately, sometimes even that isn't enough. Many of us who purchase likes and followers for any social media platform are familiar with companies such as Buzzoid, Stormlikes, Famoid, and Sproutsocial, Internet companies that have become popular over the years for selling large bundles of likes and followers, for Instagram especially, at low costs. Those looking in from the outside would see this as deceitful and wrong, calling out those who use these sites as #frauds.

However, those in the midst of it become instantly addicted after their first purchase. The high from seeing a 1,000-follower count increase almost instantly makes us compelled to keep going so we can achieve that same high. These third-party sites compete with each other to see who can give users the most bang for their buck, increasing quantity, lowering quality, but still boasting "organic likes and followers."

Contrary to what these services boast, though their services are cheap, what really happens is that people spend that $20 or that $50 on these services, causing them to feel good about themselves when their follower counts spike by thousands overnight, just to watch them all drop two weeks later, with their real fans wondering how all their followers disappeared. This causes them to buy more and more in order to compensate for their loss and to hide the fact that they bought followers in the first place. This constant cycle of buying, losing, and buying more can quickly turn that inadequate $20 into $2,000 within only a few weeks.

Brands and celebrities are more likely to buy these likes, follows, views, comments, and re-grams than anyone else, tactics used in attempts to wipe out their competition and showcase their popularity. This is one of the most common tricks in the book. Buying your first hundred or first thousand followers will allow other users to see how popular you are and want to follow you as well, eventually (hopefully) turning those first 3,000 fake followers turn into 3,000 real followers. Not only does this rarely work, but this is deceitful for real users who follow these profiles in that they become enticed by products that may actually be terrible, and can also negatively impact businesses as they become exposed for being frauds and for purchasing popularity. Attempting to trick the system can hurt profiles more than they can help because once a user is caught as being a fraud, it goes public and becomes harder for them to recover.

Everyone says commitment is the key to Instagram success, loyal followers who will always invest time into liking and commenting on posts. Buying fake followers is not the same as having loyal followers. True that it may be, the numbers are still there. 5,000 is the same as 5,000, but 5,000 real followers are far different from 5,000 fake followers. 5,000 bot followers who never engage with profiles can easily expose that account as a fraud.

If an influencer account shows 5,000 followers but only gets 5 likes per post, what the hell is going on with the others? On average, real Instagram accounts get at least 5-10% likes per number of followers, giving an account of 5,000 followers an average of 500 likes per post, not 5. Simply typing "buy IG likes" into Google will result in hundreds of links connected to "genuine and verifiable likes" for as little as one cent per like, with bundles of 100 going for as little as $3! All these sites require is your credit card information and your Instagram name with permission for them to hack onto your feed and bombard your sad profile with a shit ton of likes and followers.

They then provide you with the option of either splitting up these bought likes among multiple posts or adding them all to one post, as well as the option of obtaining all your followers at once or spread out within a span of several hours. People often go for these sporadic options when they think they can avoid having others find out that they buy likes and followers. They think that by having their followers appear sporadically, they can make up an excuse that says their "post became a hit overnight."

However, despite how much we try to make these purchased followers look authentic, we forget that people can still find out the truth by clicking on our followers and seeing that all these "magnificent followers" overnight have no profile pictures, no posts, and account names we cannot even pronounce, giving us away anyway.

Instagram users are not the only ones to utilize fake likes and followers on their accounts, using counterfeit spawns to boost popularity. In 2019, Facebook discovered that over 2.2 billion users had utilized fake accounts, and in 2013, YouTube discovered that over half its traffic were from bots and paid laborers. As more people religiously purchase likes and followers, the amounts of genuine likes and commitments begin to decrease as people realize that their influencers are actually fakes. Regardless of how many likes or followers were actually purchased, paid commitment never brings the business loyalty as real followers do. How much business can business owners actually get when over half their followers are fake? If the goal is to sell more of their products, they are going the opposite direction as bots cannot buy anything and can never help with brand dependability. The best these bots can ever do is make profiles APPEAR better than they actually are, and what good does that accomplish anyway?

In 2019, the Institute of Contemporary Music Performance executed an extensive search and found that almost all their renowned students had purchased at least 50% of their Instagram followers. These purchased bots are often sought after to give big names a push ahead of their competitors, a way to pull in new followers if people think they're more famous than they actually are. We all know how difficult it is to achieve genuine followers. Even if we think people will never find out that we bought followers, it still stands out as suspicious when we gain a suspiciously high number of followers overnight for a subpar post. No one wants to take the time to wait for a trickle of followers to appear. We all want instant gratification, and we always want to take the easy routes to get the most rewards, making the idea of buying Instagram followers that much more tempting.

Gaining fake Instagram followers usually come within a matter of an hour or two, with notices that bring that desired feeling of being famous like celebrities. These notices become energizing for a day or two, with over 1,000 new followers in less than 24 hours, until we either feel the need to buy more and more to keep up with the demand, or we see our follower counts quickly drop off when we have tried to cheap out and buy lower quality bot followers, going from 20,000 followers to just 10,000 in a week (more expensive followers aren't that much better, dropping from 20,000 to 15,000 in less than a month at the cost of more than these followers are worth).

Cheating Instagram by selling fake followers, likes, and comments have become a major business for a lot of companies, so big that Instagram began cracking down on this illegal business and filed lawsuits against companies that sold these fraudulent accounts. Still, more and more of these businesses are popping up, and people are still buying them despite the risk of having their accounts banned.

Social Media Series Limited, a New Zealand organization, sold fake likes and followers through sites such as SocialEnvy.co, IGFamous.net, and Likesocial.co, where users paid between $10-$99 every week for these fraudulent activities. In only a year, this organization made over 9.4 million dollars, in which a claim was then filed against them for "drawing in and benefiting users with promises of phony preferences, perspectives, and devotees on Instagram," violating the US Computer Fraud and Abuse Act cybersecurity law.

"Inauthentic action has no spot on our foundation. That is the reason we give critical assets to recognizing and halting this conduct, including obstructing the creation and utilization of phony records, and utilizing AI innovation to proactively discover and expel inauthentic movement from Instagram." ~Facebook

What's the point of buying Instagram followers? Fake followers never actually interact with our profiles. Imagine traveling on a cruise to Antarctica, a dream come true, posting that experience on Instagram to share with your one million followers, and hoping to receive a surplus of likes and even new followers in return. However, the next morning, you wake up with only two likes and zero comments, wondering where all your loyal followers had gone before remembering that all your followers are fake. The more we buy followers, the more we deceive ourselves into believing our followers are real, and the more we engage in activities we don't even like to please followers who don't even have opinions of their own.

Additionally, for those potential influencers hoping to get sponsored, sponsors know when accounts are fake. They can tell when users have bought followers or not just by doing a quick scan of the types of people following them, whether they are trolls and bots, or actual users with lives and posts of their own. Once sponsors discover that certain posts have been a fraud, it immediately discredits these influencers from becoming sponsored by them or anyone else.

Instagram is a platform that holds a high personal stake in maintaining their foundation as a place where users need to invest time and energy into making it big, similar to all other social media platforms. Be that as it may, a multitude of fake accounts don't really accomplish this purpose nor make people feel human or invested. Because of this, Instagram has been making efforts toward decreasing unwanted conduct and fraudulent activity, working day and night to remove counterfeit records, creating mass decreases in Instagram followers magically overnight, whenever wherever, with famous Internet celebrities going from millions of followers to only a several hundred.

Instagram has become the most popular social media platform, and not necessarily in a good way as it has also brainwashed its users. Nowadays, we scarcely even look through Facebook posts or Twitter tweets, spending roughly seconds on each one before moving onto the next. With the recent crackdown on fake purchases, companies have become sneakier when it comes to providing services that won't get banned on the platform, promoting their services as "100% organic" and "GUARANTEED to not get blocked on Instagram," which all never really last, causing increased differences in prices when it comes to purchasing followers.

For example, buying 1,000 followers from StormLikes costs roughly $12.99 while buying that same number of followers from Mr. Insta costs $35.99. Despite the claims of "organic followers," fake followers are often exposed with names similar to a keyboard, random numbers and letters with zero posts as opposed to real users. These sites to purchase followers allow us to feed our needs of wanting more.

We start off with 100 authentic followers and feel the need to have more. So, we buy an additional 1,000, hoping that would satisfy our needs and desires. However, after we get that 1,000, we are still not satisfied, thinking we'll be even more satisfied when we hit 3,000. What happens when we hit 3,000? We see others with even more, so we aim for 4,000, 10,000, 20,000 to eventually 300,000 and counting because as long as the option to buy followers exist, we will never be satisfied with the numbers we have, constantly desiring more worship and more slaves as we crave the thought of actually being famous. As we see accounts bringing in 100 likes per hour, we question whether these accounts are real, even if, in the rarest of cases, they are. What photo can be so popular that it just pours in likes by the second? Are people actually reading posts or are they just randomly liking images as a tactic for their own profiles?

#obsessed
Instagram Exposes Humanity

Human beings are social creatures, animals who pine for others to like them and worship them so they feel important. However, with the algorithm that is Instagram, only those who already have a shit ton of followers will receive likes on their posts while the rest of us become forgotten and unknown, making us feel the need to obtain those followers by any means possible in order for our posts to even mean anything. I mean, what's the point of spending so much time and effort on something just so no one can ever see it because we have zero followers, discouraging us from social media, or at least from honest social media?

Influencers looking to receive sponsors but only have four likes per post and 100,000 followers should think again. Without some sort of more authentic and loyal following, companies are less likely to sponsor someone with a bunch of followers but only one comment that says, "Great!." In addition, these bots will never share your posts with others on their stories, leaving you still unexposed to the broader IG crowd.

#instaddiction

As we see the rise in Instagram influencers, we begin to envy them and strive to be just like them, pretending to show the world that we have something worth noticing also and a strong base of loyal fans who we strive to motivate and amuse. Consequently, as we hope, these loyal supporters show their appreciation for us by liking, sharing, and commenting on our photos and videos, all the while, we, as influencers, are paid handsomely for basically doing nothing.

This idea of being able to get paid for simple images empowers influencers and micro-influencers to fabricate a notoriety that makes them stand apart from their colleagues who aim for the same themes and outlets. Most Internet-based influencers always have certain themes they swear they abide by, only because they believe those are the most popular. One of UK's most influential influencers, Zoella, aka Huda Beauty, showcases her popular life as a beauty influencer, archiving every moment of her life through beauty products and tutorials.

Internet-based influencers are often seen as having the power to drive the mentalities and support of their followers, throwing content at them daily and believing they will see them or posting content solely based on what their supporters want to see, never really getting to post what they want to for themselves.

"It wasn't until I joined Instagram in 2017 did I begin contrasting myself with others and wondering why I didn't look a certain way."

The psychological well-being of Instagram influencers is most often influenced by their followers. When influencers first open their accounts, there are already constant thoughts revolving what they need to accomplish and how they need to accomplish their goals in order to reach the status of "top dog." Their previous conceptions going into Instagram completely change when they realize they need to play to a different crowd in order to keep up with the increasing mainstream images.

#obsessed
Instagram Exposes Humanity

"When I first post something, and it doesn't get a fuck ton of likes, I become extremely disappointed and begin to doubt myself. I waste constant hours checking other influencers' pages and re-evaluate my scenario and how I can become more likeable and more entertaining."

"I let negative comments get to me, way too much, like I'm in a relationship with Instagram and constantly need its approval. One bad comment, and my day is ruined."

"Instagram has over 700 million active users and is developing each day."

"Instagram users 'like' roughly 4.2 billion posts per day!"

"Over 40 billion photographs shared, and 95 million every day!"

Having multiple Instagram accounts is common among celebrities and non-celebrities alike, with many having both genuine and fake accounts. VIPs and Instagram influencers often portray this to elevate their number of followers, meaning the more followers they can get per account, the more sponsors and cash they roll in. Significant influencers and celebrities have been known to make over $100,000 per Instagram post for doing nothing but parading around half-naked, showing young kids that this is what they need to be in order to also be famous. Some parents have also forced their kids to exploit their bodies as a means of gaining these desired followers and becoming Internet stars, forgetting what it means to be normal people with interests that don't need to be publicized to the world.

"In 2016, Instagram stories was released to showcase story highlights, Snapchat-style highlights where people can post pictures and recordings for easy access to their profiles, allowing users to pile random photos on top of each other and portraying them to the world over a period of 24 hours."

"It's a numbers game and super competitive; it's crazy how many followers and likes each person can get."

"I started by unfollowing influencers who have made me feel like my self-esteem is worthless. Honestly, I don't even know why I started following them in the first place."

"Realize that it's all fake, and stop comparing yourself to it."

"It's not real. Stop priding yourself on something that's not fucking real."

For the most part, although we are mindful of social media being fake with high standards that no one can ever meet, we still neglect to remember that when we compare ourselves to others on the Internet, we forget that the posts we portray are also not genuine while judging others for the same thing. Our insecurities continue to allow us to trick and deceive ourselves because it feels good to think, even for a second, that we are someone important, even if it isn't real.

However, the more we remain stuck in this mindset of believing we're someone we're not, the harder it becomes to break out of this pattern of loneliness. We end up believing that our fake Instagram lives are actually real, and we end up failing to be able to separate real life from this concocted life. We spend all our time and money on something that can and will never be real, and we become stuck in a mentality where we either give it all up and admit that we have been lying, or we continue holding onto this secret of being frauds.

We forget that, most of the time, the people we're trying to compare ourselves to online are fake themselves. So, what if they boast being true influencers with #nofilter? We don't actually know whether they're telling the truth. But, at the same time, we want to become like them so badly that we change our personalities and faces just to look like them, getting plastic surgery to make ourselves look better when these people we're trying to compare ourselves to have just Photoshopped their faces or are just fake accounts with stock photo faces.

"I need people who see me online to also see me face-to-face without asking themselves if a truck mauled down my face."

"On the off-chance that I have a flaw or blemish on my image, I delete it."

"If you see 3-4 pictures of me on my post, there's definitely a guarantee that I took over 100 before posting those few. I have to put my best face forward. I can't have the world seeing the ugly side of me."

"Before a photoshoot, I always take about an hour preparing myself, saturating my skin, putting extensions in my hair, perfecting my makeup, and so on. I also spend time rehearsing exactly how I want to position my body so I get my best sides captured."

#obsessed
Instagram Exposes Humanity

"Although a few of us are attempting to keep it as genuine as possible, it doesn't change how online life is mostly curated and never shows the full picture."

"We trash-talk those we follow on Instagram, but at the same time, continue following them even as we hate them."

"We allow others to pull our self-esteems down, and we know it, but we still cannot get off the Internet. We find it difficult to cut the strings despite the deadly effects on us."

"Many of us hate Instagram with every being, and we constantly feel the need to leave, yet, we feel stuck, a feeling we cannot explain because of our addiction, especially if we're 'influencers'."

"Relying solely on Instagram as a source of income is deadly. Instagram is not a job; we can't expect it to sustain us in the long run. Once Instagram is done, so are we."

"Buying Instagram followers allows us to focus our time on others things rather than just Instagram. However, even as we try, it continues to suck us back in."

"The standard of what it takes to remain on top of the Instagram influencer board constantly changes; it doesn't matter how hard we try or how authentic we remain, what people want will always change, and pretty soon, we're yesterday's news."

"We focus too much on getting others to like us and getting by based on how we look. What else do we have to offer the world? What makes Instagram that much different from Tinder?"

"What will it take for us to feel good about ourselves? Destroy Instagram?"

We know we're addicted to Instagram and social media when the idea of posting stresses us out as it takes us hours just to post one image, but the idea of not posting at the required times stresses us out even more. When people, normal people at least, post images on Instagram, it's usually just as simple as choosing an image, throwing a random caption on it, a few dozen hashtags, and posting, putting the phone aside until the next morning. The rest of us, on the other hand, begin to twitch and seize when we feel like the option of posting online becomes inaccessible to us.

We spend so much energy invested in posting that the thought of not being able to post something at the scheduled times makes us feel paranoid that we'll immediately lose hundreds of followers if we don't. We become so dependent on Instagram that we lose sleep over not being able to post, always mentally preparing our next post, and calculating exactly what's needed in order to achieve the optimal amounts of likes.

We also let our addictions drive us insane and preoccupy our minds when we check our posts and only see 5 likes as opposed to our expected 500. We allow our self-worth and happiness to be driven by the validation of others on how amazing they think our lives are even when they're not. We drill it into our minds that if people do not like our posts, then they must not like us, and the number of followers we have dictate how well-liked we are.

But do you really think these influencers with millions of followers are really liked? Do you really think the lavish parties influencers claim to throw constantly actually exist, and that at the end of the day, they're not actually just alone in their pajamas? These "million-dollar accounts" may only appear so well-loved because other users either envy them or despise them. They see them as competition as opposed to idols. We stalk profiles of people we hate more than we stalk profiles of anyone else. However, we continue checking their feeds, wondering what they have that we don't and secretly hoping they post something about their own demise.

Additionally, as we all have done many times before, we become so obsessed with our profiles being 100% perfect that even after hours of perfecting our images and captions, we still end up deleting them when we don't receive enough likes per post or when we don't receive as much as our competitors. We face daily pressure with getting more likes, seeing the feeds we follow with thousands and thousands of likes per image and feeling like we can never compete. There's this constant bar we need to uphold in order to build any kind of image in the social media world. We hold ourselves to standards we cannot meet and allow our self-esteems to become crushed by the judgment of strangers.

Because of this constant wave of insecurity, we become even more attached to the app, refusing to take breaks even as we are engaging in important or life-risking activities. Do you know how many people skydive while taking a selfie and posting it, all while in the air? Do you know how many people speed down highways while taking selfies with their heads out the windows? Do you know how many people go backpacking in the woods and attempt to take selfies with bears as opposed to running away from them?

This idea of #FOMO makes it impossible for us to stop checking Instagram, whether it's checking our progress, liking other posts, responding to troll DMs that we receive, or simply watching live feeds. It has gotten to the point where we can't even eat dinner or watch TV without having our phones in our hands, or where we can't even sit through a meeting without itching to post about our breakfast because 11am has hit. We invest too much of ourselves into our Internet and web-based lives, wanting something we know we can never achieve or lack the motivation to achieve, disregarding the events that happen in our actual lives to meet the needs of those in our online lives, and becoming agitated when people online do not like us or view us negatively.

Instagram posts are meant to make us feel shitty about ourselves, images posted by others geared toward making us feel inferior to them, from their extraordinary activities, expensive homes, and luxurious demeanor. Instagram users purposefully try to make us envy them and feel discouraged about our own lives and posts. Internet-based lives force a platform where people are forced to compare their sensible, yet, disconnected, real selves with their perfect, pristine alter egos, impeding their mental health and impressions of themselves. We are told to avoid showcasing our true selves and emotional sides because those are looked down upon, and we cannot tarnish our successful reputations online by portraying our true personalities.

Fabricating Authenticity

It's the age of 2020! Time to put forward our best Instagram games or drop off Instagram forever. This means, fantastic hues of filters, flawless live videos, pictures worth a million dollars, and the best concocted stories to portray our best selves. We attempt to deceive people about pretty much everything, from how we look to how we behave to how we speak to even what we do on a daily basis.

#obsessed
Instagram Exposes Humanity

"I only wear cute and fashionable clothes. Like, ever!"
#OOTD #instafashion #daddysmoney #iwokeuplikethis

"I'm super, super vegan! I never eat meat products at
all, except egg whites, but those don't count." #veganlife
#kalenation #animallover

"I never wear makeup. I always have a perfect and
flawless face naturally. I think girls who wear makeup are
trying too hard." #allnaturale #freshface #naturalbeauty
#bedface #itrytoohard

"Oops, I didn't know they were taking a picture of me
and my perfect pose." #caughtoffguard #hotness
#instastar #nofilter

"I love animals. I am a huge advocate of anti-animal
cruelty." #animalrides #sittingoncamel #onceinalifetime

"I always keep random products by my side. I use them
all the time!" #sponsored #whatsitcalled #loved
#awesome

"I cook at home like I'm in a 5-star restaurant. My
friend's say I'm the best chef around!" #masterchef
#justwhippeditup #noeffort

"I took this perfect picture on the first try! The other ones
are just backup in case I lose this one." #selfielife
#perfectface

"I dug up this picture from YEARS ago with my
childhood friends! I can't believe I still have them!" #tbt
#fbf #memories #nostalgia

We willingly let ourselves become bankrupt by continuing to hide our false behaviors. Research has shown that the financial expenses of influencers who buy fake followers have risen to $1.3 billion. Influencers who feel the need to show off their wide number of supporters go through extortion to get an even bigger following, paying an average of $49 per 1,000 YouTube subscribers, $34 for Facebook, $16 for Instagram, and $15 for Twitter. In one investigation, it was found that influencers of the Ritz Carlton had over 78% fake followers, P&G with 32% fake followers, and L'Occitane with over 39% fake followers, an average percentage of 20% fake followers for influencer accounts with over 50,000 followers.

Extinction of Individuality

The Internet has become a place of self-creation and self-invention, with more people using Instagram to promote and boost themselves. We live in a world where the Internet gives us the opportunity to become famous, Internet famous anyway. Look around, we see new stars popping up every day, from YouTube celebrity singers to Instagram models.

More and more people are dropping out of school to pursue their hopeful Internet careers due to how the Internet has taught us to believe that anyone can become famous and make millions of dollars on the Internet with zero to minimal effort.

We live in a time where we expect compensation for doing basically nothing but flashing our smiles or singing a poorly constructed song on YouTube and pretending to be a star. It has become so bad that even pet Instagram profiles have become so popular that they are beginning to make more money than those with normal 9-5 jobs. What pig needs to make $5,000 a month for wearing a tutu? We can't really expect to live completely off of our social media profiles, buying expensive houses and fast cars, before we realize that Internet fame only lasts a couple months before we become broke with no other prospects.

What happens when we no longer have access to Instagram? Will we still continue doing what we claim we love to do? Remember the "epic shock" portrayed by CNN, where the great social media platforms of Instagram and Facebook were shut down for 12 hours, causing a worldwide freak-out and people to become confused as to what they should do next with their lives?

People instantly feel disconnected due to the anxiety of losing all their followers, forcing them to attempt to send photos via other methods, even snail mail. We never think we rely on Instagram and social media this much until we no longer have access to them. We hear others say, "I'm not addicted to Instagram" all the time. Aren't they though? Most of us can only feel like we're part of something or are living when we are on social media, living only for others. We live and breathe Instagram, relying on it for every decision we make before acting on them.

Despite Instagram being down for only a measly 12 hours, a stretch of time that seems insignificant to most people as they'd rather be sleeping than freaking out over a stupid app, everyone else lost it. Businesses who spent hundreds on advertisements a day lost huge amounts of profit while many others saw this as the end of the world, having been so focused on this one aspect of life that they don't have a backup plan. We associate losing Instagram, WIFI connection, or even low battery on our phones with the same feeling as experiencing a breakup, heart-breaking moments that leave us wondering what we have accomplished with our lives and what we're actually capable of without the Internet. Nothing. But, this can happen. 12 hours without Instagram seems like nothing compared to 12 months without it, or even 12 years.

Don't quit your day job for your daydream of Internet fame. It's fun to chase something that probably won't ever happen for most people, but that glamorous hustle can very well one day disappear, leaving you with nothing but a crushed dream and a fuck ton of debt. Nothing is truly secure in this world, especially not our self-esteems.

Distortion Between Reality and Instagram

For most of us, social media platforms such as Instagram, Facebook, and Twitter have become our second lives, lives we wish we could live but lack the motivation and time to achieve them other than online. What makes this different from catfishing? It's not. Although our personal information (well, most of it) remain truthful, we often alter our selfie images and descriptions about ourselves to portray lives we don't actually have.

Although we realize that many people share our same habits when it comes to posting the best and deleting the rest, some of us have taken this habit to the extreme, Photoshopping every bit of their reality so much that they themselves become disconnected from reality, unable to distinguish what's real and what's not, driving their psyches toward mental insanity and false self-perceptions. How much of an obsession do we need before we realize that we are not our Internet lives, no matter how much we try to portray our Internet lives as truths?

These influencers and big names that we're so obsessed with are far from living authentic lives. From their perfect complexions to their unusual optimism, how many people in reality dance around in ball gowns everywhere they go?

Unfortunately, only a few of us are able to distinguish between what's reality and what's not, attempting to reveal this fabrication of masks that exists behind the cameras of these unrealistic portrayals of everyday life. To debunk these false perceptions, more and more people have been exposing the truth behind these posts, including posting pictures showing before and after photos of "genuine" posts known as the #Instagramtreatment, and YouTubers posting videos revealing the appalling truth behind celebrated influencers.

"Avoid accepting what you see online as truth."

"Take Instagram posts with a grain of salt, and stop comparing yourself negatively to others."

#obsessed
Instagram Exposes Humanity

> "People you see on the Internet are not what they
> appear to be."

Do people really care whether photos have been
Photoshopped, or has it become the norm? There's no
longer a need for us to resemble ourselves as we are
because we have now become forced to portray ourselves
in comparison to how others portray themselves, despite
having to color in our blue eyes green or filling in our
teeth to make them appear whiter.

As presets have become more popular in bringing in
mainstream users, more and more potential Instagram
influencers have been going this route to keep up with the
increasing demand, throwing away thousands of dollars
on presets that give their images the sparkle, glimmer, and
shine everyone craves. However, after blowing paycheck
after paycheck on these presets, people begin to lose sight
of their own image, their own vision of how they pictured
their posts. They begin to feel uncomfortable posting a
picture that no longer resembled them, feeling
uncomfortable even after obtaining thousands of likes.
We fail to realize that we put so much effort into activities
we don't even care about, throwing aside our travel
images for Photoshopped scenes and missing what we
used to love.

> "Modifying reality takes more effort than just living the
> lives we envisioned."

Still, for some people, altering photographs is the only
way they can maintain their standard of living. Take an
influencer, for example, who rose to fame through her
beautiful blue hues that captured the attention of millions
around the world. Because of this, there's that added

pressure to continue showing blue hues on her photos in order to retain her followers and sponsors that allow her to make a living on the Internet. If she were to suddenly remove these hues to portray her authentic life, many of her followers would immediately drop off as they no longer want to follow someone with subpar photos.

The idea of presets and image altering is nothing new. People have been openly decorating and polishing their images for decades to conceal the truth, whether it's with Photoshop, plastic surgery, or makeup to depict themselves as people they are not. We continue to show false depictions of the real world, living in fantasy and neglecting the raw unfiltered world. Presets add to that contorted conviction of being able to dress ourselves without effort and have others envy us for a reality that can never exist.

Stranger Approval for Self-Validation

"Our self-esteems and happiness are literally controlled by Instagram and Internet validation."

"We struggle to feel good about ourselves if the Internet hates us."

Whether it's an image of a man and his dog, an image of a young woman in a club surrounded by her girlfriends, or an image of a bride and groom on their wedding day, we all want people to like our images because it means they are telling us that they like us as human beings. We all portray ourselves as ALWAYS happy and positive, ALWAYS grateful for what we have in life, and HOW AMAZING our current lives are because we want others to give us that validation that we are well-liked regardless of how superficial our posts may be. Besides, who's going to like a post of a woman crying her eyes out from a recent breakup, a man angry and punching a hole through a wall, or a mom pissed off and yelling at her kids?

We all want to be reassured and told that what we're pursuing is actually something to be proud of as opposed to a waste of time; yet, we become angry and hostile when people do tell us what we're doing is a waste of time. We say we want the truth and honesty from others to #betterourselves, but when it comes down to it, we all only want to hear what we want to hear, seeing everything else as insults and offenses.

"Instagram and Snapchat are the most harming outlets to individuals between the ages of 14 and 25, affecting their self-perceptions as they believe the images of themselves they see online more than the images of themselves in the mirror."

Despite how much we try to tell ourselves that the images we see on Instagram are false perceptions, our brains continue to reveal what we see as truths, disguising what we know with what's in front of us. At some point in our Internet lives, we become so used to what we see online that we see them as truths and trust what we see over what we know.

Over the years, traveling has risen to the top in social media, with computerized settings being shown as significant and an identity for young adults, claiming themselves as travelers, wanderlusters, or travel experts after only having been to one international country. They are quick to show how fortunate they are, to be able to have these experiences, always portraying themselves in positive manners while also partnering with others who have the same ideals. Especially for millennials, millennials who can barely afford to live outside their parents' homes, travel has become much more than a simple 2-week vacation. Travel has become a lifestyle by which others strive to follow, bouncing from country to country and accumulating debt, never settling down until they are in their 60s, seeing career and family as second to seeing the world.

Despite what kind of traveler you are, embarking on an island hop along the Grecian waters, shopping your heart out at new and trendy stores in Milan, or meditating in the great unknown in India, these travel excursions have made it big on the Internet, causing people to travel more and more, even as they run out of money, in order to appease their followers.

In 2017, it was found that the "Instagrammability," or how well-liked a concept or theme is on Instagram, of posts rated travel inspiration as the top followed. We relish in images of notorious travelers far off in the distance of beautiful landscapes in France, images of women with their backs turned toward us and their hands reaching out to an unknown camera man, and images where you can swear these people have just stepped out of Cinderella's ball and wonder what they're doing on top of a mountain. Now, whenever you travel somewhere, you see other people attempting to re-create these same images, such as getting yelled at for having a photoshoot in the middle of a souk in Marrakesh or blockading entire roads just to reserve the Taj Mahal for themselves.

"Seeing a beautiful picture of Istanbul doesn't mean we need to book a flight there."

It becomes sickening just how many people travel now just for that photo opportunity. No one really cares anymore about exploring a new town or seeing a different country; they all just want that picture-perfect image so they can brag about it online to people who don't care. People nowadays believe that if they can replicate amazing images, then they should be popular also. They just want that attention from others regardless of whether they are warranted.

We can follow someone's #travelgram all we want, admiring their beautiful pictures and pretend lifestyles, but when asked about the country and its specifics, very few know answers beyond the scope of "amazing" and "beautiful." It's disappointing how people no longer care about seeing the world; it's more about #doingitforthegram, something that can never replace actual memories. Years down the line, we will end up looking back at our pictures and not having those memories to match the images, regretting that we have lived for the Internet rather than for ourselves.

Web-based social networking has allowed us to portray the human experience as a meme, seeing and experiencing the world through one lens and one interpretation, causing more vulnerable individuals to neglect other parts of life or the idea that life moves in different directions and with different perceptions than that of which we see on the Internet. Individuals can become manipulated by what's truly reality when their scope of knowledge is only directed through one extremely limited channel.

Despite being the true ways human beings live their lives, satisfaction, positivity, and optimism have become the only acceptable character markers on the Internet world, superficial stances on life that almost no one experiences all the time. However, failing to uphold this standard of upbeat personalities and take on life, and rather, showing the "real," or aka "troubled," side of life, can lead to a precarious and unwarranted influx of trolls and critics. The only real way to avoid Internet hatred is by concealing external emotions, portraying ourselves to the world as the "person who is never flawed" or essentially, a robot.

Surprisingly, there are quite a few amounts of people, women especially, who report feeling ashamed and guilty when they share images on social media that do not coincide with the feelings they feel on the inside. Their constant blissful images with #blessed, #beautifullife, and #lovingit do not reflect the person staring back at them in the mirror at the end of the day. We try so hard to constantly show the best sides of us on Instagram that we forget what it feels like to feel anything.

We become so obsessed with seeing images of perfect people online and try so hard to be like them for those few minutes of fame that we end up feeling lost, confused, and hopeless about our own lives. We often forget that happiness is fleeting, just like all emotions, and that unless we're programmed to be happy all the time (don't say you are because you're not unless you're artificial intelligence), it is literally impossible to be #blessed all the fucking time. It doesn't matter how #beautiful we are, how #thicc we like to have others believe we are, or how #extra we like to pretend to be when we wave around a stash of Monopoly money, we will always have to deal with misfortunes and downfalls in our lives, some more than others, but not every day of our lives will ever be perfect.

There are some of us who fabricate entire Internet lives just for that shot at Internet fame, to become that "influencer" that most of us now associate as being celebrities who do more than just try to manipulate businesses for free stuff. We change our faces and backdrops so much and literally deceive others into thinking we're important because we're too lazy to actually put in the work, using face filters to make ourselves look like supermodels when we're actually 20lbs overweight and posters as backdrops to make it seem like we're in front of the Eiffel Tower rather than in our bedrooms. The world of Instagram has become so fake that it makes it easier and easier to tease out who the frauds are. But what does it really accomplish when everything we have online are fake, fake posts, fake followers, fake likes, etc.? When nothing is real, it really doesn't matter what we post!

We can post an image of our bodies sliced in half or an image of us riding in a limousine surrounded by hundred-dollar bills and champagne, and our "followers" (more like fake followers) will comment with the same key phrases: "Yaaasss, queen!," "I love it!," or "Hahahaha," which doesn't even make any sense. Are those really enough to boost our self-validations? Knowing that a bunch of bots are liking our pictures? Does that follower

156

or that like really matter that much when we know that we paid for them? We continue talking to our "followers" like they're real people with eyes and fingers to respond, but in actuality, we're only acting stupid for talking to, well, nobody. We think we're fooling others into believing we're so popular and so famous when our engagement rates are only 0.01%, a staggering low number for someone who claims to have 6 million followers.

So, what if we have that coveted verified stamp next to our usernames? Anyone can create a bunch of fake accounts and a bunch of fake sponsorships in order to get that. It doesn't mean they deserve it. We even go as far as to fake sponsored posts, taking selfies of ourselves with random products and throwing on the hashtag #sponsored, having others think we're special and getting paid for our posts when we're just fooling ourselves. It's all about the numbers, people! You have zero friends in real life, but five million online, and suddenly your ego goes up? We live in a world where we want so much but aren't willing to put in any of the effort, resorting to fraud and lies just to achieve what everyone strives to be. Can you believe being an Instagram celebrity is worth more nowadays than being an actual celebrity?

Exploitation of Lightroom Filters

Adobe Lightroom (formally Adobe Photoshop Lightroom) has risen as one of the most popular software platforms to date as Instagram users have dependently relied on it to enhance their dull and monotonous photos. Lightroom allows us to upload our original photos and alter them depending on our likes and preferences, such as sharpening images, increasing contrasts, and even painting color hues over our faces. We can also adjust the white balance, modify exposure levels, adjust colors, fix spots, remove red-eyes, sharpen, and crop our images by using brushes to selectively adjust certain areas. Think, Photoshop, but for less skilled people.

Instagram has transformed our lives into a game of cat and mouse, in which we feel the need to be superior over others even when superiority is not warranted. We feel the need to show off our best selves to the world to the point where we also expect others to do the same. If we come across a subpar or unfiltered image of someone we know or don't know, we go out of our way to criticize them as being inferior to us, or we make huge efforts to showcase ourselves at the best places, with themed wedding destinations, unicorn parties, and pristine untouched beaches...whether they may or may not exist, just to one up them. After all, why be ordinary when you can take pictures of food at the best restaurants in town, spending hundreds of dollars on a meal just for Instagram, drink cocktails on tropical beaches just to say you were there, or abusing animals by riding on elephants, camels, and mules just to be able to brag to others about these "once in a lifetime" experiences?

Like how most of us are too lazy to generate real social media following without the use of alteration tools, most of us are also too lazy to generate our own filters, resorting to buying our presets from "Instagram influencers" who seem to have generated millions of likes because of their filters that can never represent the real world, spending thousands of dollars on filters alone in attempts to turn their minimal efforts at photography into money-worthy stock photos.

I once knew someone on Instagram who accumulated over $20,000 in debt from buying presets alone because the original ones she bought didn't bring in as many followers, so she continued buying and buying until, you guessed it, she's neck deep in crippling debt, all just for that chance to achieve perfect images that she can never truly claim as her own, resorting to begging, prostitution, and crime just to keep up with appearances, as like many other influencer hopefuls. According to the BBC and the Huffington Post, over 30% of young adults between the ages of 20 and 30 spend their lifetime salaries on promoting their online posts in attempts at those two seconds of fame, spending money they would not have otherwise for something that will probably become extinct in the next several years. We mindlessly blow all our paychecks trying to be like those we see online, trying to keep up with the ever-changing world, and trying to gain that coveted status and chance at becoming sponsored.

The irony is, we spend so much money and effort trying to be sponsored that we actually end up spending five times as much as what we would have made if we were sponsored. And when we find ourselves really struggling, with absolutely no way of continuing with our lifestyles, standing on chairs to take a restaurant quality photo of café food, buying and returning clothing we can't afford to boast our "lavish" lifestyles, and dropping our own images over someone else's face to pretend to be in places we have never visited, we delete our accounts.

"We believe life is not worth living until we can live it Instagram-style."

"We force our partners and families to pay for wedding destinations in extravagant places, like the Maldives or Santorini, just so we can have Instagram-worthy pictures on our accounts."

#obsessed
Instagram Exposes Humanity

"We spend over \$50,000 on a wedding dress, just to wear it in a couple of pictures and then never even look at the dress again."

"We manipulate our partners into proposing to us just because everyone else on Instagram is doing it, and we need to be part of the moving crowd."

We put our financial futures last because we're so busy accumulating debt by trying to achieve the impossible. That's why American and European millennials are having children when they're older and older. It's because they have spent all their time and money on Instagram that there's nothing left for them to raise a family with, putting their lifestyles of traveling the world and taking videos of themselves eating (yes, videos of people eating, called "mukbang," can generate up to millions of likes, believe it or not) over saving up for the future. Divorces happen so often because we have become so obsessed with the idea of relationships and getting a relationship rather than learning how to keep a relationship.

Those happy couples we see online are not actually as happy as they always appear. We only travel and eat in fancy restaurants because we want that chance to take that viral picture that will drive up our social media fame overnight, seeking out adventures solely for the purpose of social media rather than experiencing the interests for ourselves. This Instagram-based life is designed solely to make us feel as if wedding planning and relationships are easy, that traveling do not come with locals and tourists at popular sites, and that raising kids is the most relaxing activity in the world. We fall for these lifestyles and become motivated to try them out ourselves, just to find out that the Internet has lied to us.

"Because we keep buying fake followers and fake likes to enhance our Instagram accounts, and because we keep having to re-purchase these fake followers and likes to cover up that we bought them in the first place when these fake followers drop off, we end up becoming so addicted to covering up that we bought fake likes and followers that we don't notice how much we continue to spend on these fake likes and followers until thousands of dollars later, just to still see these fake followers and likes drop off. We take up second jobs, second mortgages, sell our belongings, steal, and other money we don't have just to keep covering up that we bought thousands of followers to begin with, until we either have to accept and admit we lied or quit Instagram."

So, we already know the vast amounts of people who spend their savings buying fake likes and followers, deceiving themselves into believing that these high numbers they have are actually real people. However, since the rise of these sites, sites created to sell people thousands of followers at low costs, Instagram has been cracking down on them and banning accounts for buying fake followers. As a result, people have turned to what we like to call "organic following," where instead of paying people for a shit ton of followers at once, we pay for services where real people help us boost our following by engaging in Instagram the "normal" way.

In other words, we pay for others to be us on Instagram while we sit on our couches and eat potato chips, waiting for magic to happen. But these services don't come cheap. These organic services can cost people up to thousands of dollars for a short one month of work. Another downside is, these services are never guaranteed, and even if they do get us 10 or 20 extra followers, they're not us, so our feeds and posts remain unoriginal and almost like we don't even own them, demolishing our chances of winning over a genuine crowd that we actually care about.

"As Low as $4 for 500 Followers!"

"100% Real Instagram Followers!"

"Purchase Instagram Followers!"

"Genuine Followers Fast!"

Adobe Lightroom contributes to the growing problem of impossible lives that people risk to achieve, including painting their own faces with paint because they don't realize that their influencers had slapped a filter on their photos. We see pictures that seem too good to be true because they are. Compare the Instagram pictures of influencers with one of their video highlights, and the person in the video seems almost like a completely different person than the one in the pictures.

Why do we spend so much effort turning our photos into a cartoon show? Everyone will know they're altered when we post them, but we continue to do it anyway and deny that they've been altered, even as we're called out for them. We become so accustomed to seeing altered and filtered images that we train our brains to believe that that's reality, and when we see real unfiltered images of people, we point those out as fake. What the fuck? No one has teeth as white as paper and waists that a baby can wrap its hand around. We see these altered images as so real that we expect people in reality to look like Instagram models, rejecting them if they don't. Imagine people altering and filtering their Tinder or dating app pictures. That is a very quick way to lure people in, yet, send them running the other direction when they see that you're not really who you portrayed yourself as online.

"Lightroom is a cutting-edge application that millions of Instagram influencers use in addition to fifty other apps to enhance their pictures."

Eventual Collapse of Instagram

Like all social media platforms, Instagram will eventually become outdated as more and more social sharing networks rise. The fall of Instagram, and even other popular social sharing platforms that currently exist like Facebook and YouTube, is inevitable, a sad truth for these so-called "Internet celebrities" and "influencers" who hope to make a permanent living from prancing around half-naked and asking for free stuff. I remember when I was a kid, people were obsessed with platforms like Xanga and Myspace, which have now become virtually unknown to younger generations.

"Trendy" platforms, as we like to call them, never last. We expend all our efforts and time rising to the top of Internet platforms that only bring us a few years of fame before the popular crowd jumps into the "next big thing." Facebook topped Myspace because of its ability to connect with others based on similar status, locations, and friends, pretty much an "acceptable" way to stalk people. Instagram topped Facebook for its ability to showcase maximum quality photos with minimal effort. But, this fame won't last. Pretty soon, another social platform will come along and dominate all existing ones, causing these influencers to become broke and homeless with no potential future prospects.

When Instagram falls, so do the interests that people portray on it. Will these food bloggers, fashion gurus, and travel adventurers continue doing the things they claim to love doing on Instagram, or will all those interests be tossed aside because they no longer have a platform to boast themselves on? Social media has become so popular because people can literally do nothing and gain everything, generating no useful skills of their own to survive in a social media-free world.

Release & Unplug

"Does Instagram make you genuinely feel good about yourself, or are you left feeling worse than you did before checking your social feed?"

"Have you ever tried to quit Instagram, just to find yourself re-activating your account days later?"

"Do you ever find yourself screaming and cursing about how much you hate the Internet and the fakes on it, just to find yourself taking and posting your own selfie soon after?"

#obsessed
Instagram Exposes Humanity

"It's easy to start. It's harder to quit."

It's an extremely difficult task when we try to quit Instagram and social media because so much of our lives are validated by these platforms. Before I quit Instagram, I had over 20,000 followers and counting, feeling validated and important, almost like a star, when I posted an image on the platform and received thousands of likes (I know, conceited). Every like and every follow made me feel like I mattered and kept me motivated to continue traveling the world, even though at one point, I questioned whether I was actually traveling for myself or to please the anonymous social media environment. The hardest decision came when I decided that Instagram was sucking up all my time; my time was spent either taking the best pictures, coming up with the best captions, or scrolling through endless other feeds and liking random pictures just so they would like mine back. It became exhausting, but whenever I saw that slight increase in following, I literally felt like my life was complete. Pathetic, right?

Eventually, I made the decision to completely delete my account and never look back. It wasn't until stepping out of that world did I realize how fake Instagram actually is, with so many people bragging about themselves when over 80% of their followers are fake, and influencers with the nerves to ask for free stuff in exchange for publicity of them in a bikini with a hidden hashtag that promotes small businesses. It wasn't until I stopped obsessively trying to capture and film myself at extravagant places did I realize how ignorant people are for prancing in front of cameras in public, or running off to different places for that perfect shot.

#obsessed
Instagram Exposes Humanity

Seriously, people take images of the dumbest things when they think they are influencing on Instagram, like lying on a sidewalk next to piles of trash or standing in front of a wall full of graffiti and calling it an "urban lifestyle." I went hiking at Zion National Park in Utah last year and, on my way back to catch the shuttle, my steps were blocked from crossing the street because two girls in sport bras and booty shorts were spread out on the road, yes, ON THE ROAD, taking pictures of each other with their butts sticking out, with the shuttle coming any minute (part of me had hoped the shuttle hit them just because of how obnoxious and selfish they were being. I mean, there were children there; they didn't need to be exposed to that culture).

When we step out of a world where we feel pressured to live life for other people or to live life only for the sake of showing others that we're better than them, we realize that we have so much more to offer the world than just our boobs and asses, and we realize how inconsiderate we have been while trying to keep up with the Internet, disregarding others and the world around us just so we can climb to the top of the influencer chain.

Nonetheless, Instagram is addicting, and it's addicting for a reason as the creators have spent time and research designing a platform people find it difficult to pull away from. From the minute we open Instagram on our phones, we are either bombarded by activity from others on our posts or by new posts from others that we can't seem to stop looking at because we're envious that we cannot come up with the same high-quality images. This continues to happen so often that, when the day comes where we decide we will not look at our phones, our anxiety will push us into wanting to because we know that there will be SOME kind of notification on it, making it difficult to step away for even a couple hours. We become so accustomed to updating our "followers" on our lives, commenting on other posts, or coming up with ideas for our next posts that we lose focus on what's important in life, spending up to 15 hours a day on a platform that, in reality, no one really gives a shit about.

We become engaged to a virtual relationship where we allow our moods and lifestyles to be dictated by social media, feeling discouraged and depressed if we are not well-liked, and only feeling optimistic and positive when someone likes our posts. We depend on Instagram to survive, proven by cases where people have threatened to kill themselves because they did not receive enough attention or to try to gain attention. Many people even fake their own suicides and mental illness just to get a few moments of fame from strangers.

When we step away from social media, we no longer have to live a life where we dedicate it to those around us. That's exhausting! We are free to do what we want to do for ourselves and at our own paces without the distraction of competition or others not liking the same things we like. We are able to spend more time with those we love and on things we actually care about instead of spending hours filming ourselves eating. We can enjoy what we eat and use the rest of that time on something else. We can now focus on generating content that we are proud of without the influence of haters telling us to stop, and we can wake up in the morning and NOT reach for that phone for once. Best of all, we can finally discover our true purpose in life even if others don't agree.

We learn to realize that remaining genuine to ourselves is more important than external validation because a life where we need to rely on others can never stay permanent as the interests of others also rapidly change. Although there is that constant fear of not staying connected with those close to us, social media is not the only way to communicate with people. When's the last time you picked up your phone to actually call someone? Although no longer a widely accepted form of communication due to chat, direct messages, and email, losing social media does not mean completely isolating yourself from the world.

"When I chose to give up social media, not only did I delete my Instagram, but I also deleted my online presence completely, Facebook, YouTube, even LinkedIn. I couldn't deal with the constant pressure and idea of having others judge me based on my online presence without getting the chance to know me. I wanted to be free from a world of cyberbullying and competition, and live more in a world where I can live life at my own pace."

Will Social Media Annihilate Human Civilization?

"Instagram is a soul-sucking creation that will eventually destroy us if we do not crush it first."

This dependence that we have on social media is SCARY! As much as we try to deny it, we live for Instagram. The phrase "do it for the 'gram" doesn't exist without reason.

#obsessed
Instagram Exposes Humanity

We have become so obsessed with trying to get that perfect shot that we fail to realize how stupid we look in public or how dangerous these acts are until it's too late. It has become an endless cycle of taking images of ourselves to show up others who aren't even looking!

I'm sure I'm not the only one who has ever tried to eat at a restaurant or relax on a beach, and suddenly, become bombarded by selfie-taking Instagrammers sticking their noses everywhere like they're the only ones who exist. Instagram has become a platform of nonsense, where people take images of pink walls and selfies while wearing fake mermaid tails and pretending to be mythical creatures. We go through extreme lengths for photos to share with complete strangers, risking our lives when we take selfies in the middle of a crowded road in New York City. Do it for the 'gram, guys. Do it for the 'gram.

Because we have become so reliant on this platform, we may end up perishing before Instagram does. An estimated 250 people die each year from taking selfies alone, all just for an Internet application. We follow movements we don't care about so we can get the attention of those who do, and for the chance to show others that we care about stuff also when all we care about is attention. The human population have become dumber and dumber as we no longer know how to think for ourselves or live for ourselves without the influence of others.

"The influencer hype will eventually come to an end, you know it, I know it. No one can sustain an entire lifestyle with no talent and a Photoshopped body. It doesn't happen in the real world! Pretty soon, these entitled influencers, who think they own the world, will face the harsh truth that they need to get real jobs."

"We have let our lives become controlled by external validations on Instagram that we now base our worth on how many likes we receive."

"We do not allow ourselves to feel good about our lives unless the Internet likes us."

"Instagram is the worst social media network for mental health and well-being. Despite the photo-based platform performing highly on means of self-expression and self-identity, it is also associated with high levels of anxiety, depression, bullying, and FOMO, or the "fear of missing out."

Instagram has gotten so out of control that any well-known online presence on the platform makes us believe that we are celebrities. We let this false fame get into our heads that, whenever we go out, we must end our days with millions of pictures that capture every moment of our awesome lives. We live in a culture where, unless we have proof through our pictures, no one will believe we did anything we claim to do. People have become so fixated with online expression over the years that the level of depression have skyrocketed as people no longer think they're good enough unless they have epic pictures.

Individuals become so obsessed with looking like the people they see on the Internet, whether real or fake, that they begin personal battles with themselves to achieve looks that are unachievable, including blowing millions of dollars on plastic surgery and suffering from eating disorders. This obsession detaches people from the real world, unaware when cars are headed their way as they pose for selfies, and neglecting their children as they have their kids take promiscuous photos of them.

#obsessed
Instagram Exposes Humanity

"The world is turning into an inexorably innovation-adjusted society, and no one can live life fully without it."

This obsession with the perfect post on Instagram has gotten so real that it is now referred to as an art when people can post the perfect image, from taking a picture of the same fucking thing 20-30 times with over 15 styles of poses to sorting through decks to get the best ones to throwing on the most magnificent filters to really enhance the sky to spending hours coming up with the wittiest captions, just to do it all over again the next day because the current day is over from all that time trying to choose the perfect image. The mentality that most people have of needing to delete images that don't generate a ton of likes within the first couple minutes is detrimental. We lose sight of the genuineness and soul that comes with posting our first image, the image we actually liked, and instead, we present ourselves to the world the way the world wants to see us.

"You're not allowed to post more than one image a day on Instagram."

"If you get under ten likes on one post, you might as well quit Instagram forever because that's humiliating and pathetic."

"If your pictures don't look the best, you need to take them off the Internet because they're shit."

"If you don't have a selfie at the Giza Pyramids, then you can't call yourself a 'travel influencer'."

"When was the last time you didn't let Instagram control your life, where you actually went somewhere awesome without feeling the need to document it?"

Instagram-based life is taking control over humanity, as over 3 billion people around the globe and over 85% of Americans have an account on top of other social media accounts. The average American has roughly six different social media accounts, with Instagram, Facebook, Twitter, LinkedIn, and YouTube being the most popular (more now given the rise of Snapchat and TikTok).

It has become so big that even pets and babies have their own social media accounts. What the hell does a dog or a baby need an Instagram account for? Not that they can use it. But, people continue to create these because they are unable to generate a following on their own, so they live vicariously through the fame of their infants and their pets, unless 4-month-old baby or a 2-year-old Labrador gets extremely upset when they only receive five likes on Instagram.

Instagrammers are always trying to brag about and show off their best selves to the world when they are actually just living in hopelessness, desperateness, and despair. We continue to live in futile ways, posting the best videos and staged images of ourselves, like having someone spit water on us to represent rain or having someone throw piles of sand on our asses to give us the "natural look," and we manipulate, in whatever ways possible, to get the most likes and comments on our feeds.

We experience the new reality as a life where we walk among others and continually compare ourselves to them, either seeing ourselves as inferior and need to change, or superior and letting our egos drive up our narcissistic tendencies. We become so obsessed, yet, then so embarrassed with the actions we engage in online, such as buying fake followers, that we either spend thousands buying fake interactions, or deleting our accounts completely if we cannot measure up or if Instagram purges are hard-bought bots. We post about our "hard lives" as an attempt to generate more drama and, therefore, more of a following when none of what we say is true. We pretend to have battles with ourselves and others just to appear controversial because people seem to follow accounts that defy the norms.

"Instagram has stirred such a war among strangers, calling each other out for faking or stealing photos, that it has become part of daily life and a compulsion."

"We become slaves to our online worlds as we are fixated with what is portrayed online, driven by our animalistic desires to want attention by any means possible."

"We are addicted to Instagram."

Confession of an Instagram Addict

"I joined Instagram during the summer of 2018, well behind the game compared to everyone else. I never really cared about Instagram or social media; I just wanted to live for myself and do the things I love without the need to share them with the world. My hobby of choice was traveling. I haven't been to many places during my lifetime, and I really wanted to experience traveling to an international country alone. It seemed like such a dream come true, a moment I never thought I would be able to experience, that I wanted to document every moment for myself to remember a time I never thought would be possible.

I remember hopping on a plane to Sri Lanka for the first time, alone, naïve to the language and culture of the country, but ended up loving every moment, from the food to my interactions with the locals to the hostel stays to the elephant rides to hiking down to see the best waterfalls in the country. I experienced the most amazing three weeks of my life on this trip, spending more time on the physical experiences than on taking pictures and selfies, leaving the country with endless memories but only a few photos.

I didn't care. I didn't stand posing for hours, trying to capture my best moments and staging moments just to make my pictures stand out as stock photos. I was too focused on living in the moment and feeling free from the pressures of modern life that time flew by, and my limited pictures appeared crooked and blurry. I didn't care. I didn't need amazing photos to showcase my time in Sri Lanka; having experienced it first-hand was more than enough.

A few weeks after my trip, I started a new job. I told my new co-workers about my travel experience, and they encouraged me to put my pictures up on Instagram. Before then, I had never even heard of Instagram. I had a Facebook account, but I rarely used it so it became outdated. Deciding to give it a try, I signed up for Instagram, opened an account dedicated to my travels, and posted the three images I had from my trip to Sri Lanka. Over the course of the next several months, I continued traveling to more places, not for Instagram purposes, but because I had fallen in love with traveling from my trip to Sri Lanka.

I traveled alone to countries like Belize, Norway, Italy, Albania, and South Korea, and I loved every minute of my adventures. Taking only a few images again from each country, I posted those onto Instagram as well. I gradually posted images on the platform as I had them, never in a rush and never caring how many likes or followers I received. After eight months on the platform, I received over 200 followers with about 10 likes per post, which is far from a lot by Instagram's standards. But, I didn't care. I continued living life the way I normally would, never focusing too much attention on Instagram and only using it to post the few images I had each time, no filter, no altering, no Photoshopping, all 100% real with maybe one or two hashtags.

A few months after that, I started dating someone who had over 8,000 Instagram followers and counting. He was portrayed on Instagram as a 'fashion guru'. I didn't even know there's an online community dedicated solely to male fashion. He was so obsessed with his Instagram profile, taking images of himself in the same pieces of clothing, only mixed up, every day, and he refused to take a day off, calling Instagram his full-time job. Wait, I thought Instagram is just another social platform where people share posts with each other when they're bored or during their down time; never did I think people dedicated their time to Instagram like they would an actual job. Anyway, this guy broke up with me shortly after we began dating because he became offended when I called his obsessive fixation with Instagram 'stupid' and told him his captions seemed pretentious.

Come on, he was posting about the beauty of the world and how happy he was literally EVERY SINGLE DAY, and whenever we went out to eat, he refused to eat until he took the perfect photo and video of his meal. His food always got cold, and he never really ate his food because he would order the 'best sounding thing on the menu' despite being allergic or hating the ingredients. Despite me despising the pretentious and delusional attitude he showed, a part of me couldn't help but compare, compare my followers to his.

How was it that I was actually living a life, traveling the world and experiencing landmarks most people would die to see, while he took pictures at the same spots and dined at the same restaurants day after day, and still had thousands of followers over me? This began to tear apart my self-esteem. I became obsessed with my own Instagram account, constantly checking day after day to see if I had received more followers. To this day, I'm still not sure whether my strong desire for Instagram followers was due to the need to feel popular or the need to get revenge on this guy for dumping me by getting more followers than him.

My first attempt at trying to boost my following was to just travel to more and more places. I booked expensive tickets to popular travel destinations all over the world because I thought that would surely boost my following. $15,000 and memories of Greece, France, Japan, Iceland, Singapore, Australia, New Zealand, Peru, Egypt, and India later, my following only increased to a mere 500. Clearly, my plan to get more followers had backfired, and I couldn't afford to keep traveling the way I was. I needed a plan B. I spent days researching on how to increase Instagram popularity and began following all the rules, from posting at the 'best' times to liking and commenting on others' posts so they'll notice me and like mine in return to stirring up controversial conversations to offering random gifts to people if they liked, tagged, and re-posted my photos.

However, all that got me were lack of sleep, even less money, and my followers even began unfollowing me because they found me annoying and/or hated me for bashing on the profiles of well-loved influencers. I became desperate. Nothing I did was good enough to obtain those desired followers that I desperately wanted. I was beginning to lose hope.

Then, one day, I came across an article that featured an Instagram fitness influencer who was exposed for having over 50% fake followers that she bought online, followers that are Internet bots sold by companies in bulk to give Instagrammers all the numbers but none of the engagement. The influencer defended herself by saying that she only bought followers as a marketing scheme to obtain followers because people would rather follow accounts with higher numbers. I never finished the article. As soon as I found out that there's a quick and legal way to gain tons of Instagram followers, I went for it, never taking the time to think through the consequences my actions would cause.

I quickly Googled 'buy Instagram followers' and was surprised to find out how many results came up, with prices ranging from $0.01 per follower to $1,000 per month for 'organic' followers, whatever the hell that meant. I was surprised by how easy it was to buy an entire Instagram following account. Part of me knew this was wrong. I shouldn't be buying followers, right? What happens when I get exposed for also being a fraud? But, the temptation was too delicious. I wanted those numbers. I needed those numbers. Still plagued by my conscience, I found one of the cheaper services, a whole 5,000 followers for just a mere $30, typed in my credit card information, and with my eyes closed, I clicked 'submit' before my conscience took back control over me and made me change my decision. When I finally opened my eyes, I saw my payment confirmation and a note stating that I would receive my followers within the next several hours.

Barely two hours later, I checked my Instagram, and my following had gone from a mere 500 followers to a whopping 8,000, even more than what I had paid for. Of course, these services always give you more than you ask for to account for drop offs. Whatever the reason, I couldn't believe what I was looking at, a whole 8,000 followers. Granted, I know that number came from my credit card and that they were all fake, but just looking at that number gave me a sensational thrill I haven't experienced before: power. Any decently smart person would be able to click on my newly found 'followers' and quickly point out that these followers are all fake, all accounts with no profile pictures, long-ass names with strange characters in them, and 0-2 posts on each of their accounts.

However, I was banking on people not looking too much into who my followers were and more on how many followers I had. I know, from experience, that people tend to not really care who's following you; they only care that people are following you. They look at your number, your posts, and move on, never really taking the time to investigate your profile because, well, they have lives.

Despite knowing my following was fake, I still pretended that I was hot shit. I pretended that I had a following of thousands of people who actually cared about my posts. This not only allowed me to brag to those I knew, but it also allowed me to take pictures of my daily life and travels as if I was actually someone worth noticing on the Internet.

I began to do the very things I hated, posing in public, taking selfies in public, pretty much everything we would normally do in the privacy of our own homes, I did in public. I had no shame. I even went as far as to buy more and more followers, never seeing my number as high enough, and even going as far as to strategically plan out how I bought my followers, only buying several hundred at a time and spacing the delivery times out so only a handful would show up on my account at once to make it seem more genuine. I thought I was outsmarting the system. I thought I had uncovered a secret that millions hadn't already tried before. However, my 'brilliant' plan was missing one crucial element: engagement.

Soon, people started getting suspicious, suspicious that the number of likes I was getting and the number of comments I was receiving did not match up, ratio-wise, to the high number of following I had. I had over 12,000 followers but only a mere 10 likes and 2 comments (if even) per post. A normal account with over 12,000 real followers would easily obtain hundreds, if not thousands, of likes and comments per post, or at least more than 10. My account was beginning to look fishy. It wasn't until one friend began digging into my account and trying to expose me did I really begin to take action. I soon learned that not only can you buy followers, but you can also buy engagement, i.e., likes and comments, both at different costs. Likes usually cost about $10 per 100, and comments about $30 per 50. I had already spent over $600 buying my followers and couldn't really afford to spend more on likes and comments.

However, I also couldn't risk having my account exposed and lose everything I had bought. So, with my eyes closed and credit card in hand once again, I bought 500 likes and 50 comments per post, every post, including the 220 past posts on my feed, just in case people decide to scroll down to see my pitiful history. I couldn't risk having them see that jump, from 2 likes per post to 500 only after a short amount of time. That would be too sketchy. Thousands of dollars later, I was finally able to fill all my posts with numbers that looked less suspicious, unless of course, people searched through those who actually followed me versus those who were fake.

Despite being in massive debt, I still saw this as not enough. I needed more. I wanted more. I ran out of vacation days to travel to more places so I began staging local areas around me as 'must-visit' destinations, where I would stage backdrops and drop endless filters on top of them to make my images seem more attractive. I also continued buying followers and likes whenever I heard that Instagram is purging fake accounts, a frequent purge they do once in a while to remove and expose phonies like myself. The more followers I lost, the more followers I bought back, a constant waste of money and trap I could not get out of.

This cycle, plus my continued addiction with buying Instagram popularity, eventually turned into my profile having over 100,000 followers, over 10,000 likes, and close to 500 comments per post, every post. I became so broke that I had to open up a whole new credit card just to cover these costs. Like all Internet stars, I pretended that I was a celebrity and deserved to be noticed wherever I went. I pretended I had sponsorships, taking pictures next to branded products with #sponsored.

No one ever called me out again. Some people believed that I actually had as many followers as I claimed to have. Others just didn't care enough to ask. Soon, my newfound lifestyle came to a halting end when I finally realized how much money I was feeding into this never-ending lie. It got to the point where I just couldn't continue this lifestyle anymore. By the end of all this, I was close to $100,000 in debt, spending close to $100 per post, just to keep people from finding out the truth. Shortly after, I deleted Instagram completely, never looking back, watching all that money I had wasted go down the drain as I went from being a nobody to being an Instagram fraud to being a nobody in debt. On the bright side, with all my fake followers, my number ended up exceeding that of the fashion guru's. I guess I won. Right?"

#obsessed
Instagram Exposes Humanity

#obsessed
Instagram Exposes Humanity

#obsessed
Instagram Exposes Humanity

www.ingramcontent.com/pod-product-compliance
Lightning Source LLC
La Vergne TN
LVHW042335060326
832902LV00006B/179